The
Third
Pole

ཀ།འཛོམ་སྐྱིད་
ཡང་སྐྱེ།།

The Third Pole

ཁ།འཛམ་གླིང་ ཡང་རྩེ།

Compiled by Guo Xin

Translated by Wang Hao

China Intercontinental Press

Contents

Foreword

Zhang Yiwu

The TV documentary *The Third Pole* has been a popular program and hot topic among viewers since it was broadcasted. It was released to wide international acclaim and has been regarded as a Chinese TV documentary which has gained significant international recognition. TV and Internet broadcasts have spurred wide interest in the documentary, and it has been gaining exposure through international media organs.

The relevance of this documentary can be understood in a larger context. In the past few years, treatments of Tibet have been a focus of attention for global society. As a unique part of China, Tibet has attracted numerous Tibetophiles who are enthralled by its unique natural environment, humanistic tradition, and cultural-historical background which contrast sharply with contemporary metropolitan lifestyles. Yet stereotypical impressions seem to result from clichéd accounts of Tibet which often attempt to highlight Tibet's mysteriousness and special history. The contrast between Tibet and other regions is intentionally magnified while firsthand experiences of Tibet's here and now are often absent. This poses a challenge in providing authentic accounts of the Tibetan people as they are, as people living their lives under their contemporary conditions. We find *The Third Pole* significantly different from previous documentaries about Tibet through its strenuous efforts to gain insights into Tibet, leading to a "rediscovery" of this land and its people. Though a documentary of only six episodes, *The Third Pole* nevertheless provides

insightful depictions of Tibetan people's everyday life, showing situations in which common Tibetan people attend to their daily business and capturing their stories with sensitivity. The sweep of this documentary's camera presents viewers with authentic pictures of Tibet's natural and human environment and specific individuals living therein. A striking feature of this documentary lies in its faithful representation of ordinary people's lifestyles at the "Third Pole," which is the Qinghai-Tibet Plateau as seen through an anthropological lens. This TV documentary shows us how Tibetan people live in harmony with nature in an extreme environment, immersing us in the unique charms of Tibet. *The Third Pole* has a grand subject, which is the "Third Pole" as a whole, but the audience approaches it through many specific stories, each of which serves as a portal to one aspect of the subject, thus giving a holistic view of Tibet's people and natural environment. In Tibet's extreme environment, people have settled on an optimal lifestyle that this documentary shows in an ordinary yet most amazing way, opening a space wherein the audience can admire the sublimity of human life in this world. It is a song of humanity; it is a song of nature.

By showing us the harmonious relations between man and nature, this documentary provokes thoughts on an important theme of today's progress-oriented Chinese society. This series' authentic documentation coincides with an important issue of our time: how are we supposed to achieve harmonious coexistence of man and nature amid a new round of industrialization? How are we supposed to "conform and contribute to the course of nature?" *The Third Pole* tells stories with its camera, stories about how people follow nature's course while making contribution to nature's diversity. Global concerns about animal rights and welfare are addressed, while the relationship between man and nature is examined. While most films are about human beings, this documentary features man and nature, presenting them in their complementary roles: nature comes alive through man's presence, and man assumes more sublime qualities because of nature. Thirty years of rapid economic growth has brought China to a transitional point where common people, especially young people are expecting spiritual uplift. People have broken free from a lifestyle prescribed by industrialization to seek an uplifted life and to create harmonious relations among people and between man and the natural environment. Tibet provides an example of how such uplifting is made possible; it also provides an example for global recognition of ethnic and cultural diversity. Each of the stories in this documentary has its own implications and values; they are meaningful at both the local and global levels.

The Third Pole is a successful attempt to tell China's stories using a TV documentary as a globally accessible narrative mechanism. It uses internationally recognized discourse to clear language barriers and to enhance cross-culture communication while giving credit to China's "subjective status" and the true value of Tibet as a Chinese autonomous region. Stories happening in Tibet constitute a part of China's overall story. A unique feature of this documentary lies in its representation of these stories by means of globally recognized camera language and expressions, wherein lies its capability of global transmission. All these have contributed to the unique charm of this documentary, holding promise for its reception by a larger international audience, bringing Tibet and China closer to other parts of the world, and ultimately winning global recognition of and respect for China's stories.

It is a good idea to integrate the rich content of *The Third Pole* into a book which is not only a transcription but also an extension of the documentary: it includes verbal accounts of the episodes, behind-the-scenes stories, and further explanatory notes on Tibet's natural environment, history, and culture. Whatever is included in the documentary is also found in this book, supplemented by written accounts of what cannot be easily conveyed through audio-visual media. This book is not just an outgrowth of the documentary but also a cultural product with its own value. Both the documentary and the book enable us to look far into the sky over Tibet, admire the great highland mountains, prize the life force of living creatures, and appreciate the fortitude and good nature of human beings.

May 8th, 2015

In Search of the "Third Pole"

Zeng Hairuo

What is the "Third Pole?" There is a clear answer to this question: the Qinghai-Tibet Plateau. It is the highest point on earth, also known as the Roof of the World, so it is given the appellation "Third Pole" by analogy with the North and South Poles. Its "polar" status can be further understood in terms of its glaciers, altitudes, and climates. Yet this documentary is not so much about factual analogies as it is about people who live at the "Third Pole."

The "Third Pole" is the Roof of the World, but only a few people live on the "ridgepole." Extreme alpine features are tempered by the existence of lower altitude landforms. Going downhill, one experiences the four seasons, travelling through frigid and temperate zones, subtropical and even tropical areas. This is what we call the "staircase of the earth," upon which the basic conception of this documentary is grounded.

The environment of a region can tell about its people, and that is why we have seen vastly differing lifestyles on the Plateau. In a place less than 100 kilometers from Mt. Qomolangma as the crow flies, we filmed a story about Sherpa men gathering honeycombs on a cliff. Many local Sherpas were daunted by its dangerous height, but a persistent man we met insisted on having a try. Then, nine men spent a whole day trying to collect honeycombs from a bee nest. They worked 200 meters above two converging rivers, and what was worse, the bees attacked before they barely started.

Our cameraman, who had been trained to work on steep mountains, suffered bee stings and had many lumps on the skin. He felt nauseous but persevered and finished the job. Back in our camp that evening, he had more than 100 stingers removed from his skin. This happened at a relatively low altitude of 2,000 meters.

At the altitude of 5,100 meters, the upper limit tolerable for permanent human habitation, we filmed the story of people herding their sheep across a vast frozen lake to find pasture so their sheep could survive before the Tibetan New Year. In order to show life forms in extreme environment we carried out underwater filming, a technique that posed dangers in such a setting. First of all, the air pressure felt by the cameraman working under water was equivalent to that at sea level. A dramatic air pressure drop was felt the moment he surfaced; it was like stepping from sea level right onto the altitude of 5,000 meters. It was a severe challenge to one's blood pressure. Secondly, there was only a small opening on the ice which meant that the cameraman could not surface whenever he wanted, and he would be in danger if he couldn't find the opening. Thirdly, conditions were windy and the temperature was minus 20 degrees Celsius. Any wet surface became frozen the moment our cameraman came out of water. Despite the deadly cold and air pressure change, he always offered to make another try to achieve a better shot.

We assumed that a 100,000-kilometer journey by car would cover all the "stairs" of the Qinghai-Tibet Plateau but realized, upon completion of this project, that we should have planned a one-million-kilometer trek, or an even longer distance. What impressed us most were the grasslands, the cornerstones of Tibetan culture and the locales that best demonstrated the cooperative spirit among living creatures. Making adjustments to cooperate with other creatures in demanding climates constituted an important feature of survival on the "Third Pole." It was pleasant, joyous cooperation which we called the "dance in unison" of man and other living creatures.

We filmed a story about two brothers and their racehorse, a well-known champion that was getting old. Horserace festivals were important holidays for Tibetan herdsmen and most of the jockeys were 7- to 8-year-old children. Both brothers loved horseracing, but only one of them was chosen to run the race. Coming of age was accompanied by cheers for one and tears of another. It was a somewhat cruel yet heartwarming story: a child hoping to race on a horse that had grown old.

We filmed stories about people and their sheep, about Tibetan mastiffs, yaks, antelopes, wolf puppies, and black-necked cranes. What we wanted to tell was something more than a give-and-take relation between humans and animals; it was rather a relation of coexistence and mutual inspiration, rooted in one's deepest beliefs—a "dance in unison."

Other themes like "song of the land," "cycle of water sounds," and "forest whispers" focused on how different environments shape people differently. But the story lines only scratch the surface: people on their sojourns in Tibet experience wondrous, miraculous, and mystical things. Frankly speaking, we saw remarkable things once in a while, but for the most part we lived a humdrum life during a long movie-making year.

If we intended to turn up exotic stories to satisfy our curiosity, we would have been daydreaming. I remember asking some local herdsmen to confirm my bit of book knowledge about Tibet, and they would invariably show a good-natured smile and tell me: "I've never heard anything like that."

Sometimes I tell others cautiously that I was in Tibet for one year, but what I saw most of the time was familiar things, not wonders. That is the truth. Those are the familiar things we saw in everyday life, things which haunt my dreams but slip back into the dark realm of unconsciousness when I wake up. The Tibetans are kind-hearted, hospitable, smiling people; they are devout but unassuming, humorous but not frivolous; they love food and drink but do not indulge in extravagance; they are loving parents but they are not possessive of their children; they make money to support their families but do not work outdoors all year round.

Each time I visited a Tibetan family, they would always treat me to a cup of butter tea, saying that the delicious tea would keep one energetic for a whole day. In our society, consumer goods must be diversified, and people's expanding desires must be satisfied. In Tibet, however, the butter tea could be a life-long drink, and one could always find joy and satisfaction in it. Holding a cup of butter tea, I felt myself standing on a mountain peak, my heart becoming light and capacious and my eyes looking into a farther distance. It dawned upon me that maintaining a kind, peaceful, and unblemished heart was more important than finding a great mountain or grand lake. And that was the "Third Pole" we eventually discovered.

On the peak of a mountain where rivers originate, one sees rivers and alpine ranges extending beyond the horizon and robust lives coexisting in mutual respect. These are what *The Third Pole* documents.

April 27th, 2015

On the peak of a mountain where rivers originate,

one sees rivers and alpine ranges extending beyond the horizon

and robust lives coexisting in mutual respect.

These are what *The Third Pole* documents.

The
༄༅།འཛམ་གླིང་ Third
ཡང་རྩེ།། Pole

WHAT IS TAKEN UP WITH EFFORT
CAN ALSO BE PUT DOWN WITHOUT
RELUCTANCE;
EARTHLY PROSPERITY DOES NOT
SURPASS SUCH A HANDFUL OF SAND.

LIFE'S COMPANION

The Qinghai-Tibet Plateau, with its main body embraced within Chinese borders, is the most recent yet highest highland to rise from the earth's crust. Most Asian rivers have their headwaters on this plateau where the average altitude is more than 4,000 meters. The annual average temperature of its interior is below zero degrees Celsius. This is the highest point of the world, known as the "Roof of the World," or the "Third Pole" besides the South and North Poles.

Unlike the secluded South and North Poles, this is a place rich in human activities, a place inhabited over generations by multiple ethnic groups. There's an 8,000-meter drop between Mt. Qomolangma (the Everest) and the low plains and valleys, so the life habits of wild animals,

conditioned by such radical variations in altitude, are rather different from those in other areas. A wonderfully mysterious relationship has come into being between the local inhabitants and the wild fauna. People's respect for heaven and earth and their love for life bring a sense of security to animals. People in turn find spiritual gratification from their peaceful coexistence with the animals.

The "Third Pole" features landforms ranging from snowy mountains, glaciers, and grasslands to heathland. At the foot of the snowy mountains, however, there is a large expanse of virgin forests in the eastern part of the plateau. Down below the forests, the highland gradually descends into valleys with congenial climates and fertile farmlands.

Gongbo'gyamda County
Tibet
3,600
meters above sea level

Gongbo'gyamda County | 3,600
Tibet | meters above sea level

Under the jurisdiction of the city of Nyingchi, Gongbo'gyamda County is located to the northwest of Nyingchi in the middle reach of the Yarlung Zangbo River Valley. The Sichuan-Tibet Highway and the Nyang Qu River run across the town, which slopes from west to east with great mountains and crisscross valleys on the north and the south. The Tibetan phrase Gongbo'gyamda means "mouth of the great low valley."

BLESSINGS OF THE LAND: DOBGYE AND TIBETAN MACAQUES

Below the thick forest of Gongbo'gyamda lie the remains of a deserted village. Dobgye goes across it every day to come to the foot of the mountains frequented by wild animals. He hollers toward the forest, and a group of macaques will run toward him and surround him in excitement. These monkeys, 2,000 in population, are Tibetan macaques, a species unique to China. Dobgye takes out a bag of wild fruits and gives the macaques a treat.

Dobgye was born to a hunter's family. Fascinating hunting stories are still circulating in the village where he lives. Those renowned hunters used to be heroes, but they have already changed jobs since the government made this piece of land a nature reserve. Now, Dobgye's job is to protect this forest and the animals therein.

More than a decade ago, over 50 monkeys broke into Dobgye's village to plunder their crops and refused to leave. According to Dobgye, it was sowing time, so there were no crops yet. The villagers had just plowed the land and sowed the seeds, but the macaques dug out and ate the seeds before they got a chance to germinate. Most of the villagers had once been hunters, and an all-out war seemed inevitable.

Before hunting was banned they would have killed any monkeys they chanced to meet, but this time they made the least likely decision: they left their village to the monkeys. Many families relocated to make a new start, and many people began to make new career plans.

Having lived in their new homes for some time, however, people find themselves living a better life than in the mountainous areas and the land here is a lot more fertile. The government's initiative to develop tourism brings an increasing number of tourists who contribute to the local people's income. People take this as a blessing in return for giving their land to the monkeys. For Dobgye and his folks, this land is full of memories of home, but now it has become heaven for the monkeys.

In April, peach trees are in full blossom across the valleys of Nyingchi. These flowers are known far and wide. The Peach Flower Festival, a tradition started in 2002, is gaining popularity. The monkeys love the peach flowers too. Dobgye is bringing more fruits and peanuts lately, for he knows that the monkey mothers need more nutrition to foster their young in this season when monkey babies are born in large numbers. He says that each of these active, playful creatures deserves to have a name of its own. Other people also bring these monkeys candies, walnuts, and fruits on festivals and other special days. Dobgye hears from people of the older generation that the Tibetan people are descendants of macaques that had bodhi-hearts.

Story of the Macaque Who Turned into a Human Being

According to Tibetan myths, the Monkey God married a female raksasa (demon) on the prompting of the bodhisattva Avalokiteśvara, and the couple thus became the ancestors of man. This story is not only circulated among the Tibetan people but also narrated in Rgyal Rabs Gsal Ba'i Me Long (The Clear Mirror: A Royal Genealogy) and the murals of the Potala Palace and the Norbulingka Monastery. Folklore has it that the cave in which the Monkey God once lived is located in the Gungbort Mountain near Zetang. The Tibetan word ze means "to play" or "to have fun" while tang means "plain," so Zetang means the place where the descendants of the Monkey God and the raksasa play and have fun.

The Tibetan Macaques (Macaca thibetana)

Tibetan macaques, commonly known as "big blue monkeys" or "grey monkeys," are a species of the genus Macaca. As the largest member of the macaque family, an adult Tibetan macaque can be 58 to 71 centimeters tall and weigh 25 to 30 kilograms. Tibetan macaques are categorized as "wildlife under second-class state protection" according to China's "List of Wildlife under State Protection."

The adult Tibetan macaque has brown fur, a large head, and a hairless and flesh-colored or dark-grey face. Newborns have silvery black fur which turns brown at the age of two.

Although its Latin name indicates Tibetan origin, the Tibetan macaque is not native to only to Tibet. They mostly live in sub-tropical jungles between the altitudes of 800 and 2,000 meters. They are widely distributed in Sichuan, Tibet, and Yunnan.

Tibetan macaques live on hilly, rocky terrain in broad-leaved woods. They live in communities and feed on wild fruits and young leaves. They are adjusted to cold climate and appear to be comfortable with human presence.

Xainza County | 4,750
Tibet | meters above sea level

Xainza County | *4,750*
Tibet | meters above sea level

People's readiness to live with wild animals is part of the plateau's local culture. More than 800 species of birds choose to live on the Qinghai-Tibet Plateau, and that makes it one of China's wild bird havens sheltering some rare bird species.

BLACK-NECKED CRANES: ANGELS OF THE PLATEAU

Under the jurisdiction of Nagqu Region, Xainza County is located in the central part of Tibet between Mt. Gangdisê and Serling Co, the largest lake in North Tibet. Serling Co, surrounded by an emerald necklace of 23 satellite lakes, is the center of a cluster of lakes. All these lakes are said to be part of a great water body that existed millions of years ago. Lake Co Ngoin, among all the planet lakes, has a "bird island" which serves as a rest stop for migrating birds. Tens of thousands of Mediterranean brown-headed gulls arrive here each summer after a journey of more than ten thousand kilometers. They are a grand view. The Serling Co Black-Necked Crane Reserve is a national wet-land nature reserve located at the juncture of the counties of Xainza, Nyima, Nagqu, Amdo, and Baingoin. This piece of land, 18,936.30 square meters in area, was made a national nature reserve in 2003 to protect black-necked cranes and their breeding sites.

On one of the many lakes across the northern Tibet grassland, a crane couple is building their nest, cleaning the surrounding space, and taking turns to sit on their two eggs, the fruits of their love. Black-necked cranes are the only crane species living in highlands. They are a rare species like giant pandas. Once they become a couple, they become life-long companions. Together, they forage and walk around the lake and take care of their nestlings. Baby cranes follow their parents soon after they are hatched. These grey, fluffy young birds look quite different from their parents. It will take them quite some time to learn to forage on their own. In the next two to three months, they must learn to survive in harsh environments. In fall, the crane parents must make the decision to only keep the stronger of their two children, for the moment is soon to come when they must fly over the snowy mountains. Weak young cranes won't be able to survive the arduous journey and make it to their new home.

Lhünzhub County
Tibet

3,860
meters above sea level

8848m
8000m
7000m
6000m
snow line
5000m
4000m
3000m
2000m
1000m
500m
200m
0m

Lhünzhub County, under the jurisdiction of Lhasa, is situated in the Pengbo River valley of the Lhasa River's upper reach in central Tibet. Sixty-five kilometers away from the city of Lhasa, the county is a thin strip of land stretching along a north-south axis. Mt. Kala, an offshoot of the Nyainqêntanglha Range, divides the town into a southern and a northern part. Lhünzhub is full of natural beauties and tourist attractions.

One day, Dawa from Punchog Ling Village found an injured black-necked crane while herding her cattle. The crane had lost a leg and many feathers. He struggled to stand on the remaining leg. Then Dawa finds that the crane has been anxious and irritable lately. She also notices that many of the cranes living across the northern Tibetan grassland are flying to the valley and gathering on the farmlands of her village as well as a few neighboring ones. Dawa realizes that, well-fed as he is, the crane feels lonely and misses his own kind. Dawa then sets out to look around in the neighborhood while herding her cattle, hoping to find another injured crane to keep him company. But there isn't any injured crane to be found.

Dawa and her husband apply a mixture of ghee and penicillin to the crane's wounds every day. This is a cure they have known since childhood. Yet they disagree on what to do with the crane. Her husband believes they should keep the crane in order to take care of him, but Dawa wants him to have company. Dawa says that she knows of a place where people take care of the cranes and she is considering taking the crane to these people. Her son goes to school in Lhasa, and she wants to have his opinion on this because he is well-informed. The young man says that the crane can receive professional care at the animal rescue center. He thinks that the crane should have a prosthetic leg. Dawa cannot imagine how her crane will look like with a fake leg.

What happens in the next few days, however, convinces her not to hesitate any longer. Dawa is shocked to see a spiteful stray dog attacking the cranes in their gathering place. She drives the dog away, but one of the cranes has already been killed. Dawa buries the crane in grief. She is disturbed: where healthy cranes live in such danger, there's no telling what may happen to her crane. She decides to call the rescue center. The rescue staff arrives with their truck. Dawa lifts her crane in her arms and puts him in a big carton box. She has prepared 50 kilos of wheat in case that her crane doesn't like the food at the rescue center. She asks the staff to remember to add some sand to the wheat, and some of their regular feed too if they want. The truck drives off, and Dawa is in tears. She will miss her crane.

The black-necked cranes are flying back to their hometown in north Tibet. Dawa wishes that her crane can join these birds someday. Soon, Dawa meets a new friend, another injured crane, who now crouches in a corner of her house. Dawa feeds him and caresses his feathers.

Black-necked Cranes (Grus nigricollis)

Black-necked cranes are the only crane species living on the highland. They are an endangered species under first-class protection in China. They are mostly distributed in Tibet, Qinghai, Gansu, Sichuan, Guizhou, and Yunnan. A small number of them are also found in India, Bhutan, and Nepal.

Black-necked cranes live on lakes, marshlands, and riverbanks on highlands between the altitudes of 2,500 and 5,000 meters. They feed on algae and sand grains as well as plant leaves, tubers, and rhizomes. An adult crane stands 110 to 120 centimeters in height and weighs 4 to 6 kilograms. It has white-grey feathers, a long neck, and slim long legs. Except for a dark-crimson spot and a few hair-like feathers on top of its head, the upper two-thirds of its neck are covered with black feathers, hence its name black-necked crane.

Their population is small because their home, the Qinghai-Tibet Plateau, is a cold highland where changeable climate and extreme conditions result in a high mortality rate of their young. China has established nature reserves to cover their breeding sites and their migration route and destination. More than 6,000 cranes, or 75% of their total population, fly to Tibet in winter, and more than 4,000 of them raise their children here.

Ge-sar rgal-po (*the epic of King Gesar*), the longest epic ever written in history, tells of a flock of noble and dutiful birds charged with the responsibility to take care of the king's royal steeds. These birds are black-necked cranes. As one of the favorite birds of Tibetan Buddhist followers, they are an auspicious animal usually painted on Tibetan-styled cabinets as well as in thangka paintings, a thousand-year-old Tibetan art.

EACH CREATURE DESERVES TO BE RESCUED: THE HERDSMEN AND THE WOLVES

On the Qinghai-Tibet Plateau, people's love for animals brings them so close to wild animals that their sheep are often mixed with antelopes. Yet such intimacy is also dangerous. The government's environmental preservation efforts have given rise to the increase of wild animals including wolves. Domestic sheep are often attacked by the wolves and killed by deadly bites on the neck. The wolves have caused great losses to the herdsmen. A recent wolf attack has left quite a few sheep with fractured bones. These sheep may die tomorrow because they are too weak even to eat grass. Saddened and angered by their loss of more than 20 sheep, a few herdsmen have called the police. The government will compensate for their losses, but the roaming wolves remain to be a thorn in their side. The herdsmen say that the wolves are growing in number and will become more menacing if their population is not

controlled. So many sheep have been killed—the wretched creatures! Sheep farming will be more and more precarious with so many wolves out there.

The herdsmen find a litter of stray wolf pups on a snowy day. Although they have been constantly troubled by wolves, the herdsmen take the pups into their tents. The lady of the house feeds the pups with the remaining flesh of a sheep killed by wolves. They take pity on these pups which are sure to be killed by the cold weather in a single snowy night if they do not reach out a helpful hand. These Tibetan herdsmen believe that each creature deserves a chance to be saved.

In China, The Qinghai-Tibet Plateau has the largest number of nature reserves. In Tibet alone, there are 47 nature reserves that cover 1/3 of Tibet's territory.

Nature Reserves in Tibet

Tibet takes up the main portion of the Qinghai-Tibet Plateau. With an average altitude of more than 4,000 meters, it boasts a unique ecological and geophysical environment. Since the peaceful liberation of Tibet, the Chinese government has made great contributions to Tibet's ecological development and biodiversity preservation, with commendable results.

Tibet is one of the most biologically diversified regions in the world with unique types of landscape and vegetation. Currently, it is home to more than 9,600 species of wild plants, 798 species of vertebrates, and about 4,000 species of insects. More than 1/3 or 125 of the species on the national list of key protected animals are found in Tibet. More than 600 higher plant species and 200 terrestrial vertebrates are found only in Tibet. Over the years, detailed and comprehensive surveys of Tibet's fauna and flora have been conducted by national and local experts, and preservation plans have been made with measures taken accordingly.

Tibet's regional government has been increasing financial input into wildlife protection since the 1970s, and has established no-hunting areas in the habitats and breeding sites of wild animals. Nature reserves of various kinds have been established in Tibet since the 1980s to form an optimally structured network for wildlife protection. Human activity for economic development is strictly prohibited in established reserves to restore eco-equilibrium. Efforts have also been made to provide effective protection for the habitats and breeding sites of endangered species, natural landscapes of value to scientific research, and important fossil sites for geological and biological studies.

Zadoi County | 4,200
Qinghai | meters above sea level

Zadoi County | *4,200*
Qinghai | meters above sea level

8848m

8000m

7000m

6000m
snow line

5000m

4000m

3000m

2000m

1000m

500m
200m
0m

Bharal (blue sheep), those cliff-edge dancers, like to nap in precipitous spots when tired. A large flock of bharal like this is sure to attract their natural enemy, the snow leopard. The snow leopard, the reputed "king of snowy mountains," is a mysterious animal rarely found below the altitude of 4,000 meters.

EACH CREATURE DESERVES TO BE RESCUED: DR. GEORGE SCHALLER AND THE SNOW LEOPARDS

The county of Zadoi is situated in the southeastern part of Yushu prefecture and the southwestern part of Qinghai Province. It borders Tibet to the south.

Dr. George Schaller, born in Berlin, Germany in 1933, is a senior conservationist in the Wildlife Conservation Society (WCS). As one of the world's preeminent field biologists, Dr. Schaller has been engaged in research and protection of wild animals since the 1950s. He travels throughout Asia, Africa, and South America, and studies a number of large endangered species ranging from lions, tigers, and gorillas to giant pandas and Tibetan antelopes.

Dr. Schaller is a leading biologist promoting the study and protection of snow leopards across the world. This time, he travels a long distance to Zadoi to study the snow leopards here. In the mountains, he is the first to discover a makeshift den of a leopard. Soon he finds some hairs in a rock cave higher above. The snow leopard has rubbed against the rocks to leave his hairs and scent. This is a day of fruitful gains,

but drawing inspiration from the conduct of Tibetans, Dr. Schaller decides to move on for fear of disturbing the peaceful life of a good friend.

In fact, the globetrotting Dr. Schaller was amazed by an incident two days ago. He takes out a plastic bag with a tiny black caterpillar inside. He says that he saw large numbers of these caterpillars on his way from Yushu to Zadoi. He was amazed to see many cars pulling over and people getting out to pick up those caterpillars which would later turn into moths. Basins and pails in hand, the people picked them up carefully lest they should be crushed by the vehicles passing by. These caterpillars were then set free again in the grass far away from the highway.

Here, the herdsmen see snow leopards quite often. They can even clearly spot the dens of these leopards. They point out one of these dens for Dr. Schaller. Dr. Schaller finds it easy to identify that location and he believes a clear picture can and must be taken of it. They continue their search in the mountain. Dr. Schaller thinks that they have made the right assumptions, but there are also other possibilities. Though he has missed seeing the snow leopards, Dr. Schaller is not disappointed. For him, the study of snow leopards is not entirely dependent on an encounter with them. The most important of his wishes is that his leopard friends can live a carefree life.

Tibetan Snow Leopards (Panthera uncia)

The snow leopard is a wild animal under first-class protection in China. It is the renowned "king of the snowy mountains" living near the snow line.

Snow leopards are an endangered species found in the Western Chinese provinces and autonomous regions of Sichuan, Tibet, Qinghai, Xinjiang, and neighboring mountainous areas in central Asia. Their habitats are found at altitudes between 2,000 and 6,000 meters, and their population is believed to be smaller than that of giant pandas.

Snow leopards have grey fur with black spots all over. Their long tails are covered with long fluffy hair. They are the most beautiful members of the genus Panthera.

Snow leopards are solitary and nocturnal animals most active at dawn and dusk. Alert with keen senses, they are agile climbers and jumpers who hunt antelopes, bharal, gorals, and deer. Sometimes they also hunt small animals such as hares and ground squirrels. An individual snow leopard lives within a relatively fixed home range and often takes long hunting trips. It usually travels through an area along a winding route and comes back along the same route after many days.

Snow leopards are economically valuable in some countries. Their pelts are sold at high prices on the international fur market. Doctors of traditional medicines in many countries believe that their bones are a cure for arthralgia and rheumatism. These are the reasons why snow leopards are being hunted and poached. They are most likely to be captured with iron traps placed by poachers on their habitual routes, thus leading to their endangered status. What's worse, the decreasing population of bharal is catastrophic to their survival. Only a very small number of snow leopards are successfully bred in zoos across the world because it is hard for them to acclimatize to the changes in humidity, temperature, air pressure, and sunshine at lower altitudes.

The snow leopard is the most unique animal of the alpine highlands of Asia. Successful protection of snow leopards is a crucial part of the world's alpine fauna protection efforts.

BEINGS THAT LIVE IN MUTUAL RESPECT:
A NYI MAMA'S GREY MASTIFF PUPPY

Anxiety pervades the black yak-wool yurt of herdsman A Nyi Mama in Zadoi, Qinghai. His family is talking about their elderly dog.

"This dog can no longer guard the house"

"That's because he feels lonely."

"Without dogs we can't keep our cattle safe."

"We need to keep two or three more dogs. Dogs are like people. They need company."

A Tibetan mastiff stands at the entrance, as if he understands what his master is saying. "That dog is wailing all day long," says A Nyi Mama. "I'm so distracted that I cannot focus on herding." The family decides to find a companion for the dog so he won't be too sad. A Nyi Mama, the man of the house, leaves home on his motorcycle to look for a suitable mastiff.

A herdsman's mastiff is not just a dog; it is the guardian of the house. It is said that a purebred Tibetan mastiff can fight three wolves or a leopard. It is strong-willed and understanding. The herdsmen believe that if the Tibetan mastiff is to be called a dog, it should be called a heavenly dog.

In another herdsman's home A Nyi Mama sees a mastiff, a grown one, but A Nyi Mama wants to have a younger, smaller mastiff. Apparently, this one does not win his heart. He will continue to look around. There are several criteria for selecting a mastiff, such as thick fur, large paws, and mighty appearance, but the first impression counts more than anything else. This is the so-called predestination. A Nyi Mama comes to a professional breeder whose Tibetan mastiffs have attracted many buyers from other towns. A Nyi Mama sees a mastiff of a fine breed, but he doesn't want to buy it. His trip continues.

Money is not a consideration for A Nyi Mama because he keeps more than 300 yaks, but he really wants to get a mastiff for reasons other than money. Tibetan mastiffs are rarely sold between herdsmen. In their culture, good mastiffs are priceless. A Nyi Mama remains empty-handed after many trips, but he knows that haste leads nowhere; one should patiently follow the predestined road toward the final encounter.

One day, he meets a man on the road who says he keeps a few Tibetan mastiffs. A Nyi Mama follows this man to see his dogs. It seems that the right one has been waiting for A Nyi Mama; it only needs to show up at the right moment in the right place. At the first sight of the grey puppy, A Nyi Mama feels as if they have known each other for years. It's a heavy, large-pawed puppy of fine breed. The man decides to give the puppy as a gift to his sincere, earnest guest. A Nyi Mama is overjoyed and thankful. He says he will check the calendar to arrange a welcome. He cannot take the puppy home right now according to tradition. Instead, he must pick a good date for a formal welcome.

On an auspicious sunny day, A Nyi Mama brings a hata to the man and brings the grey mastiff puppy home. In his tent, he gives the puppy's nose a slight burn with fire he gets from the stove. This makes the puppy a new member of the family, and he is named Gyasug. The old mastiff has finally got a companion. Only through such respectful treatment can two creatures become equal beings.

Tibetan Mastiffs

Native to the Qinghai-Tibet Plateau, Tibetan mastiffs are also called "songpan dogs" and "snowy mountain lions." They are strong and fierce. An individual Tibetan mastiff is about 120 centimeters tall with a strong physique and thick fur. It is said to be the only ancient rare breed that has survived.

Primitive Tibetan mastiffs live above the altitude of 3,000 meters in cold alpine regions and Middle Asian plains. They are found in Mongolia and Nepal as well as the Chinese provinces and autonomous regions of Qinghai, Sichuan, Gansu, Tibet, Xinjiang, and Ningxia.

Tibetan mastiffs are omnivores which prefer meats and tangy foods. They are adapted to cold but not hot climates. They have keen senses of hearing, smell, and touch, but dull senses of sight and taste. They are loyal, understanding, strong, and fierce dogs with a good memory, but they are aggressive toward strangers.

Tibetan mastiff breeds may look different because of their living conditions. The premier breed has been shaped by conditions in Nagqu, Tibet. The harsh environment of the Himalaya Range has given them tough looks and contributed to their noble, kingly temperaments.

Tibetan mastiffs are called "heavenly dogs of the East." A historical saying goes that a real mastiff comes from a litter of nine. Their loyalty to their masters has made them ideal guard dogs of nomadic tribes.

Amdo | 4,800
Tibet | meters above sea level

Amdo | **4,800**
Tibet | meters above sea level

Under the jurisdiction of Nagqu Prefecture, the county of Amdo is located on the north and south sides of the Dang La mountain range in North Tibet. Amdo is a large county with a complex terrain of vast grasslands and numerous rivers, lakes, and glaciers. Mysterious, snow-covered Geladaindong Peak and the headwaters of the Yangtze River make this place look like a beautiful crystal palace of thick snow and permanent ice. The perilous peaks of Dang La loom in multiple poses and shapes. Cultural relics, beautiful landscapes, and unique customs of Amdo contribute to its charms. With a developed transportation system, Amdo serves as the northern gateway to Tibet.

A number of shepherds live and keep large flocks of sheep at the foot of the great mountains in Amdo. Before the eyes of a matron, a solemn ritual of sheep selection is taking place while the sheep are being milked. The matron is ready with her colored bits of cloth, and a man throws a rope lasso at the sheep. Life is changed forever for those lassoed. Bits of cloth are tied to the ears of the sheep chosen to continue to live in their flock, as a sign that they are forever exempted from slaughter. These are called "freed sheep." Many Tibetans believe that illness and bad luck can be avoided by freeing a sheep.

ANIMALS MAY FEEL HAPPY TOO: THE STORY OF TSEWANG AND TSERING

Lhasa, the capital city of Tibet, is situated on the northern bank of the middle reach of the Lhasa River, a tributary of the Yarlung Zangbo River. As a renowned ancient city with more than 1,300 years of history, Lhasa is the political, economic, and cultural center and transportation hub of the Tibet Autonomous Region.

In the city of Lhasa, an old man, stick in hand, walks slowly downstairs. He walks out of his home with a sheep. His name is Tsewang. He and his sheep punctually show up on the street of Lhasa every day. He has named his sheep Tsering. He says he has been taking the sheep everywhere with him since it was only a small lamb. Tsewang takes a circumambulation trip every day, and the sheep is always following him. As he gets on the bus, the sheep will also jump onto the bus and stand by him quietly. The circumambulators are the people Tsering sees regularly. Sometimes he stops abruptly and quietly fixes his eyes on these people.

Eight years ago, Tsewang bought this sheep 49 days after his wife passed away. The sheep Tsering is a symbol of his fond memories of his late wife, as well as his wishes for a lucky turn on the wheel of samsara for the deceased. He will keep the sheep, he says, till the last day.

He believes in the intimacy between man and animals. Animals don't speak, he says, but they feel happy living with a kind master.

Tsering is sheared once a year. Tsewang's daughter gathers the wool to stuff the quilts for her father. Enough wool has been saved for two quilts over the past four years. Tsewang wants to have a look at his new quilt. He smells the wool and looks satisfied.

Eighty-year-old Tsewang has been too sick to take his circumambulation trips lately. His daughter tells him that the sheep has been bleating a lot because Tsewang cannot go outside. She wants to walk the sheep, but Tsering refuses to go out with anyone other than Tsewang, including his daughter.

Concerned about his and Tsering's future, Tsewang decides to call a family meeting. All his other daughters are now back home.

"Dad," asks his daughter. "You are most worried about the sheep, right?"

"Besides you," says Tsewang.

"Shall we take the sheep to our hometown in Rinbung?" asks another daughter.

"No," says Tsewang. "He can't adapt. He's gonna die there."

"The sheep takes the place of Mum," says yet another daughter. "Dad can't allow him to be sent anywhere." Tsewang nods in agreement.

Now a granddaughter proposes to send the sheep to the Norbulingka Zoo. She believes that this is the best solution because Tsering can live in his own pen as the only sheep there. And they can visit Tsering on Saturdays and Sundays. Yet Tsewang is afraid that the sheep won't like it there because people don't do circumambulation in the zoo and the food is not good. They haven't reached an agreement on Tsering's future, but the old man is in good spirits, and his daughters are having a good chat. Everyone is happy at this family gathering.

The Tibetan New Year, one of the most important Tibetan festivals, is around

the corner. Tsewang's daughter and granddaughter are cleaning the house. They are also giving the sheep pen a thorough cleaning. The New Year is a time for family gathering and feasting. A lamb's head is the most important dish at the banquet, and a sheep statuette must be placed on the table for worship. Tsewang lives in a big happy family with his children and grandchildren. The family is dancing joyously, and the house is full of cheerful singing and chatting. The children are singing drinking songs. They offer the first cup of wine to Tsewang and wish him health and longevity. At the height of the partying, Tsewang remembers Tsering. He stands up and goes to visit Tsering with New Year delicacies. He ties a piece of new cloth on Tsering and says to him: "We have both grown another year older. I wish we can be still together this time next year. I wish we can live a hundred years to see more of fall harvests."

"When I was young," says Tsewang, "elderly people told me that they mostly freed fish so their spirits could flow down the river when they died. If you freed a sheep, he would carry your spirit on his back and swim downstream with the current."

The old man comes to the top of the mountain with Tsering. Many white ladders are painted on the crags on the backside of the mountain. It is said that such a ladder is painted so that the spirit of one's deceased family members can use the ladder to climb up to heaven. To save a life is to build a ladder. Tsewang enjoys looking down at Lhasa from here, and so does Tsering. In the Tibetan language, Tsering means longevity.

Freed Sheep

In Tibet, sheep with colored bands on their necks are often seen near Buddhist monasteries and in herdsmen's homes. The masters of these sheep are all devoted followers of Tibetan Buddhism. These sheep have been freed, and hence exempted from slaughter. They are called "freed sheep."

For a herdsman, freeing a sheep can help avoid misfortune while accumulating merits and virtues, so it is an important, serious event. He can randomly pick and free one or a few sheep. An urban resident, however, has to buy the sheep he intends to free. Buying a sheep about to be slaughtered is recommended because this adds to the special implications of freeing it. Freeing a sheep is not just about setting it free; it involves a series of rituals. Usually, one takes the sheep to a Buddhist temple to do circumambulations. Then a red cloth band will be tied to the sheep before it takes leave on its own. From now on, it is a freed sheep in the real sense. Sometimes, however, a freed sheep under the influence of a strong religious atmosphere may understandingly follow the people in circumambulation, as if to show its thankfulness.

Freed sheep are lucky not only in that they are exempted from painful slaughter but also because they will be taken care of by the circumambulators. These people will feed them so they won't have to walk around looking for food. This may be the reason why they also join in the circumambulations, thus becoming a sight unique to Tibet.

Circumambulation and Prayer Wheels

In Tibetan Buddhism, circumambulation is a religious activity in which people walk along a circuit and pray. Followers of Tibetan Buddhism believe that circumambulation is equivalent to sutra chanting. It is the best form of penance and the best way to avoid misfortune and accumulate merits and virtues. Some circumambulate sacred mountains and lakes, some holy cities and monasteries, and still some stupas and mani cairns. Prayer wheels are available in all the Buddhist monasteries in Tibet to maximize the benefits of this merit accumulation method. Many people also carry their portable versions of prayer wheels which they keep turning in their spare time. On the street or in Buddhist monasteries, many people in traditional Tibetan robes are seen spinning their own prayer wheels of various styles. This can be seen almost everywhere in Tibet. Circumambulation embodies a practitioner's expectations for his future and the next life.

There are large prayer wheels and much smaller ones which can be held in one hand. The smaller wheels, which are made of gold, silver, or copper, are also called hand prayer wheels or mani wheels. The main part of a prayer wheel is a cylindrical wheel with copies of sutras and mantras inside and the six-syllable mantra embossed on the exterior. Most prayer wheels are exquisitely crafted items embossed with mantras and animals and birds. Some are inlaid with coral and precious stones which add to their value beyond their religious significance. The cylinder is affixed with a weight on a chain or cord so that a slight rotation of the handle will set the weight in motion and keep the wheel spinning. Practitioners believe that the faster the wheels spin the quicker their merits and virtues are accumulated.

Though small wheels turn faster, practitioners believe that they are incomparable to larger ones which contain many more sutras and mantras. Turning a large wheel generates many more merits and virtues than spinning a small one. That's why they take time to turn large wheels besides spinning their hand wheels from time to time. Large prayer wheels are mostly found in and around Buddhist monasteries. Rows of large prayer wheels fixed on wood spindles are an imposing, mysterious sight.

A large prayer wheel, made of copper or wood, can be one meter high with a diameter of more than 40 centimeters. While copper wheels show the color of copper, wood wheels are mostly painted red and covered with silk, sheep skin, or cowhide. These wheels can usually be turned by a hand sliding over it. Turning of the wheels means the sutras and mantras inside are being recited.

The Tibetan New Year

Tibet has many festivals which vary according to region. The New Year, for example, is celebrated on October 1ˢᵗ of the Tibetan calendar in Nyingchi, formerly known as Gongbo. The Gongbo New Year is celebrated by banishing demons, inviting dogs to banquets, eating gyida, carrying water on the back, and giving offerings to the goddess of harvest. Yet the residents of Tsang long ago designated December 1ˢᵗ of the Tibetan calendar as their New Year. At any rate, the Tibetan New Year is the most important and most celebrated of all Tibetan festivals.

In most parts of Tibet, the New Year falls on January 1ˢᵗ of the Tibetan calendar and roughly coincides with the Lunar New Year of the Han Chinese. Due to calendric differences, the Tibetan New Year and the Lunar New Year may be celebrated on the same day or set apart by a few days in between. The New Year festivities have strong religious implications because many Tibetans are Buddhist followers.

It is said that before the Tang Dynasty, Tibetans celebrated the New Year when the wheat was ripe. The culture of central China, including the calendar, found its way to Tibet following Princess Wencheng's arrival. This gave rise to the mixed use of ancient Tibetan, Han Chinese, and Indian calendars, and by the Yuan Dynasty, a unique calendar had come into being involving theories of tiangan (heavenly stems), dizhi (earthly branches), and wuxing (the five elements). This is the Tibetan calendar that is still used today.

In Lhasa, people begin to prepare for the New Year in December. Khapse, a local delicacy made with ghee and flour molded into various shapes, is cooked in every household beginning in mid-December. Each family also prepares a five-grain container called chemar bo, and fills it with tsampa, wheat grains, broad beans, and chuoma. These are further decorated with ears of highland barley, cockscomb flowers, small bits of ghee, and two thin pieces of colorfully decorated wood representing the sun and the moon. Fried khapse and carefully-prepared chemar bo are placed before Buddha statues as offerings. Shrines and furniture are carefully cleaned and auspicious drawings are made with tsampa on cleaned kitchen walls or the ground in front of the door. Each family gathers around the table on December 29th to enjoy a meal of guthuk, or Tibetan dumplings. Some of these are stuffed with stones, wool, charcoal, and hot pepper. A bite on any of such dumpling is invariably followed by cheerful laughter. After the meal, the whole town turns out to participate in the demon-banishing ritual. On the first day of the New Year, housewives get up before dawn to fetch lucky water from the river. The lucky water is used to cook a gruel that is eaten with other foods, and then everyone in the family dons his or her best to usher in the New Year.

The first day of the New Year is for family gathering. People get up early in the morning, put on new clothes, and give offerings to Buddha and gods. Then, with chemar bo and barley wine in either hand, they offer their New Year wishes to one another. Beginning from the second day, people pay New Year calls to their friends and relatives. Tibetan opera are performed in cities and the countryside, and people also engage in a series of recreational activities including guozhuang circle dance, tug-of-war, horse racing, and archery.

The ༄།།འཛམ་གླིང་ Third
ཡང་རྩེ།། Pole

Kind thoughts are the best
companion.
Only in the company of kind
thoughts is one free from care
and confusion.

HOMETOWN

On the surface of the earth, the temperature drops by one degree Celsius for every 150 meters in altitude. The Qinghai-Tibet Plateau, with an average altitude of 4,000 meters, is colder than any other region at the same latitude. Its high altitude, however, also brings more sunshine that compensates for the lack of warmth. Various plants grow tenaciously to add to the colors of the plateau.

Lhasa | 3,650
Tibet   meters above sea level

Lhasa's streets are bustling with activity even on winter days. This city, situated on a river plain, has a total annual sun exposure of more than 3,000 hours, or 8 hours and 16 minutes a day. That is a half again as much as China's eastern regions and two times more than the Sichuan Basin, hence its name "the city of sunshine." Here the pace of modern life exists alongside ancient customs.

Morning begins with a cup of sweet tea for many people of Lhasa. This is a

beverage brewed with black tea and milk. One gets a cup, sits on his usual seat, and lays out change on the table: miscalculation is never a concern. A good chat takes place even between strangers. The change on the table gets mixed, and people become friends sharing news over cups of tea. Now to eat a bowl of Tibetan noodles before a day's work begins in the beautiful sunshine.

Sweet Tea of Lhasa

The sweet tea is a special component of Tibetan cuisine culture with a history of more than 100 years. It is brewed with black tea and then mixed with sugar and milk or milk powder. It is a popular drink thanks to its agreeable sweetness, nutritious content, and fragrance of milk mixed with the aroma of tea. Today, sweet tea is not just a drink but an integral part of Tibetan culture.

It is long since the Tibetans formed the habit of tea drinking, but sweet tea comes from foreign lands. There are two versions of the story about how sweet tea came to Tibet. One story goes that afternoon tea was brought along by the invading British armies. Many Tibetans under the influence of the British have since made sweet tea a part of their daily life. The other story tells of a large number of Kashmirian refugees who became the first cohort of Muslim newcomers during the reign of Emperor Kangxi of the Qing Dynasty. These people sold sweet tea to make a living.

Sweet tea is very popular in Tibet with teahouses found in every corner of Lhasa. Tea drinkers fill the sweet tea houses of various grades in nameless alleys as well as in the vicinity of the Jokhang Monastery. The Laoguangming Teahouse in a small unnoticeable alley of the Pargor Street is the best example of a sweet tea house.

A sweet tea house is used as a leisure-time establishment by the locals as well as a place to take a rest after circumambulation. Friends in twos and threes sit around a table on which they spread their change. The waitresses fill each cup and then collect the sums due from piles of change. The tea drinkers have leisurely chats about everything ranging from politics to life, religion to domestic affairs. Each group of tea drinkers now becomes a temporary social circle. The sweet tea houses can be seen as an embodiment of Lhasa's vitality and street culture.

Tibetan Noodles

Tibetan noodles are an indispensable part of traditional Tibetan cuisine. They look just like those from the central plains of China, but taste quite different. A first-time eater will find the noodles soft on the outside but tough on the inside as if they were only half-cooked. This happens to be one of the peculiarities of Tibetan noodles.

Tibetan noodles are a type of wheaten food of the Qinghai-Tibet Plateau, and that's probably why many people think the noodles are made from highland barley. Actually, they are made from regular wheat flour instead.

Ready-made Tibetan noodles are cooked and dried and put aside for use. To prepare a bowl of the noodles, one only has to warm the dried noodles in a pot of yak soup. Ladle the noodles out into a bowl of yak broth and add some cubed yak meat with a bit of Tibetan hot sauce, and a bowl of tasty Tibetan noodles is ready to be served with a saucer of pickled turnips.

The essence of Tibetan noodles lies in its hot broth. A fragrant and agreeably fatty soup with chopped scallion pieces makes a bowl of palatable noodles. Cooked with yak bones but no additives, the broth is nonetheless extraordinarily delectable.

Chentang | 2,040
Tibet | meters above sea level

8848m
8000m
7000m
6000m
snow line
5000m
4000m
3000m
2000m
1000m
500m
200m
0m

Chentang | 2,040
Tibet | meters above sea level

Lhasa's congenial climate is influenced by its mountain setting. The Himalayas, the highest region on earth, is a world of ice and snow. Large deep valleys hidden in the mountains serve as channels to bring in warm and humid air currents. It is humid here with full sunshine.

Chentang is a township under the jurisdiction of Dinggyê County of Shigatse Prefecture, Tibet. It is located in the southwestern part of the county of Dinggyê on the southern slope of the middle Himalayas. On the southeastern side of the Himalayas are precipitous valleys and turbulent rapids. Here diverse wild fauna and flora live and grow in large virgin forests. Chentang became a part of China's Qomolangma National Nature

THE HONEYBEES' GIFT IN RETURN FOR HUMAN TOLERANCE AND AFFECTION

Reserve in 1989.

Sherpa farmers are transplanting rice seedlings in one of Chentang's valleys. These tribesmen mainly live in Tibet, Nepal, and India. When ripe, the crop they are planting will grow rice ears shaped like chicken feet, hence its name "chicken feet millet."

Here lives a species of honeybees called the Himalaya cliff bees. As the largest honeybees in the world, they can fly above an altitude of 4,000 meters to find hardy flowers. Their nests, usually more than 2 meters in diameter, hang high on the most perilous cliffs in the valley. A large nest that has never been touched by honey collectors hangs quietly from a cliff 200 meters above the roaring waves of two converging rivers.

More Sherpa than people from any other nationality have reached the summit of Mt. Qomolangma. They climb high mountains each year to collect honeycombs, not so much for the honey but to fulfill a divine mission.

Today, a few Sherpa men are talking about plans to harvest beehives.

"Will you be available, brother Samden?" asks one man.

"How high is that?" Samden asks back.

"About 200 meters," the man answers.

"That's a dangerous height," Samden says thinking. "I've got too much work to do at home. I can't go."

"You've got old parents and young kids to support. What can you do if something happens?"

Even the most experienced honey collectors are fearful of that cliff. They say the cliff is perilous. It is indeed very dangerous because there's no place to hide from the angry bees. Bee stings may cause one to black out abruptly. Death is a sure thing if one gets seriously stung and falls into the rapid torrents below.

"This is the most dangerous place I've ever seen," says Nyima.

Despite the dangers, their sacred mission motivates them to take the risk. As far as they remember, only two or three honey collectors have climbed up that cliff.

Bamboo sticks they cut on site are used to make the tools. Then they light torches to drive the bees away, which is the most important step. The Himalaya cliff bees are the most aggressive and poisonous of all honey bees. Smoke must be prepared before the bees are aware of their presence, or there will be hell to pay.

It begins to rain unexpectedly as they are preparing the torches. The torch is out and the smoke is gone. The whole colony is furious even before the men touched their nest. Without protection from the smoke these men will be attacked by thousands of bees, and that is exactly what happened to the elderly honey collectors in the past.

The rain is becoming heavier and the second torch is also extinguished. Heavy rain adds to the ferocious torrent below and the wind is becoming ever stronger in the valley.

They are trying to light a third torch, and if they fail, they will have to quit. They won't be able to fulfill their plan when it gets dark.

They light yet another torch, and the honey collector lowers himself down to the bee nest on a rope. He moves a large basket under the nest and pokes at the beehive with a bamboo stick. Swarms of bees are gathering on the hive and some land on the honey collector's face and hands. At any rate, he has successfully obtained large chunks of honeycomb. "Everyone ready—go!" shouts Nyima excitedly. They pull the rope to get the honey collector back to the top of the cliff.

The combs they collected must be processed before the night is out in order to produce the best quality beeswax. This is their sacred mission. This is the China-Nepal border area, and Nyima will sell his bee wax to customers in Nepal in order to buy daily necessities.

Katmandu | 1,370
Nepal | meters above sea level

Katmandu | 1,370
Nepal | meters above sea level

Katmandu, the capital of Nepal, is an ancient city with a history of more than 1,000 years. It embodies the ancient Nepalese culture with its fine works of architecture and its wood and stone carvings. Steeped in pluralistic religious culture, Katmandu has more than 2,700 temples of various sizes. It is the world's Buddha statue manufacturing center.

Here the precious golden beeswax the Sherpa men risk their lives to collect is molded into Buddha statuettes. Buddha statues made by using Himalaya cliff beeswax have a finer and shinier surface.

8848m
8000m
7000m
6000m
snow line
5000m
4000m
3000m
2000m
1000m
500m
200m
0m

Pé Town | 3,700
Tibet | meters above sea level

8848m
8000m

7000m

6000m
snow line

5000m

4000m

3000m

2000m

1000m

500m
200m
0m

Pé Town | *3,700*
Tibet | meters above sea level

Under the jurisdiction of Mainling County, Nyingchi, Pad County is located at the corridor which opens onto the great Yarlung Zangbo Valley. In Pé Town, another corner of the Himalayas, the bees take on a totally different look. According to the locals, the presence of a bees' nest is a token of good luck for the family living in that house.

A man is playing games with his children in a courtyard. The bees in the nest beneath the eaves are still very peaceful. They may be a bit stirred up when the man of the house chats and laughs loudly over cups of wine. But they have never really attacked their landlord.

One day at the turn of fall to winter, the bees are suddenly gone, leaving behind a large chunk of honeycomb. The man of the house climbs a ladder to collect the bees' present for his family. He works with great care to make sure that the nest is not destroyed so the bees will come back next year as expected. Without any effort the family gets to taste the sweet essence of nature. Such a present from these wonderful creatures is given in return for the family's tolerance and fondness. The Himalayas have fostered not only the most ferocious but also the most generous honey bees in the world.

The Himalaya Cliff Bees

The Himalaya cliff bees, living in the Himalayan foothills, are the largest honey bees in the world. Their nests are built on cliffs a few hundred meters high, hence their name.

Cliff bees generally live on cliffs between altitudes of 1,000 and 3,500 meters. They are seasonal migrants that fly to low warm altitudes in winter and cool alpine areas in summer. A worker bee can be 17 to 18 centimeters long, a few times larger than her counterparts of other subspecies.

Risking their lives and braving the stings of hundreds or thousands of bees, honey collectors living in the Himalayas will climb up rope ladders to high cliffs to collect honeycombs in the honey collecting season in spring and fall. The primitive tools and the traditional skills they use have remained largely unchanged over the years.

The entire honey-collecting process takes about three hours with the collectors playing collaborative roles. They smoke out the bees first, and then climb up the cliffs using rope ladders. They move close to the nest and quickly collect it by using simple tools like wood sticks. Now the enraged bees will attack the collectors, but these agile and skillful men can still finish their job calmly and unhurriedly.

The honey and beeswax they harvest will be reprocessed, and the beeswax will be made into bricks, each weighing about two and a half kilograms. The villagers will keep some of the honey and wax for their daily use and sell the rest in order to buy food and other daily necessities.

The honey collectors in the Himalayas believe that honey is a blessing of the gods, so to collect honey is to find that blessing by following in the footprints of their ancestors. They never kill all the bees for their comb but leave a portion of it to grow again. This is a centuries-old tradition that not only allows the colony to keep growing but also ensures that the traditional way of honey collecting is handed down.

The Sherpas

The Sherpas are a cross-border ethnic group living at the China-Nepal border areas. They are the reputed "porters of the Himalayas." The Sherpas, or "eastern people," are descendants of the Dangxiang Qiang people, an ancient Chinese ethnic group that moved westward. With a population of 40,000, Sherpas mostly live in Nepal and about 1,200 of them live in China's Tibet Autonomous Region. Living across borders, Sherpas have tenaciously adhered to their unique culture in their long and complex historical development.

Sherpas live in compact communities in highland areas 5,000 meters above sea level. Under the influence of the natural environment and their traditional culture, their lifestyles and religious traditions are similar to those of the Tibetan people. They have no family names but do have given names which resemble Tibetan ones. They have their own language but no writing system, and Tibetan is commonly used. Tibetan Buddhism is their religion.

Living in highland areas, many Sherpas are engaged in farming and husbandry, including cattle herding and wool processing. The major crops they grow include corn, potatoes, chicken feet millet, buckwheat, and beans.

Long-term living in highland areas has shaped their unique physiological features. They have astoundingly large lung capacities and a higher content of hemoglobin in their blood. They have been working as guides and porters for mountaineers since the 1920s. Sherpa individuals are found in almost all the mountaineering teams that climb Mt. Qomolangma because of their industriousness, fine physique, resistance to oxygen deprivation, and good mountaineering skills. They are the ethnic group with the largest number of mountaineers who have successfully reached the top of the Qomolangma and who have died trying. The Sherpas have made memorable contributions to man's history of climbing Mt. Qomolangma. Today, providing guide and logistic services to mountaineering teams from all over the world has become the Sherpa people's major source of income.

Nyêmo County | 3,800
Tibet | meters above sea level

8848m

8000m

7000m

6000m
snow line

5000m

4000m

3000m

2000m

1000m

500m
200m
0m

Nyêmo County | *3,800*
Tibet | meters above sea level

Under the jurisdiction of Lhasa, Nyêmo County is located on the northern bank of the Lhasa River's middle reach in south-central Tibet. It is 140 kilometers southwest of Lhasa. In the Tibetan language, Nyêmo means wheat ear. With a long history of incense manufacturing, Nyêmo County is one of the locations best known for making Tibetan incense.

PRESSING AND PRINTING AS DHARMA PRACTICE: DORJI'S TIBETAN PAPER

Pink flowers are in full blossom on a gentle gradient near the Yarlung Zangbo River in Nyêmo. Sheep seem to abhor these flowers, which they never eat. These are spurge flowers with a fearsome name in Chinese—Langduhua, or "wolf-poison flowers."

Though poisonous, the spurge can be put to special uses, and it is a useful plant for Dorji. Working with the patience of a farmer, he has cleared a piece of land to grow this "wolf-poison grass" with its beautiful flowers.

Poison is found in the plant's root, the part Dorji needs. Dorji digs up these spurges and removes their leaves and stems. The roots are then peeled, shredded, cooked, and mashed with a stone. Dorji makes the cooked and mashed roots in to a pulp by a traditional artisanal process. Pieces of paper made from this pulp are put in the courtyard to be sun-dried.

The Lhashö village, where Dorji lives, has a paper-making history of more than 1,300 years. "This is a legacy of our fathers," says Dorji. "I will do my best to carry down this craft."

Dorji slowly smoothes out each piece of dried paper and carefully removes it from the wood frame. This kind of paper, with spurge as its main ingredient, stands the test of time because it is tough, pliable, worm-proof and hardly discolors.

Dêgê County | **3,188**
Sichuan | meters above sea level

Dêgê County is situated to the northwest of the Garzê Tibetan Autonomous Prefecture of Sichuan Province. In the Sakyapa monastery of Dgon Chen there is a sutra printing house, the Dêgê Parkhang, which is well-known for its rich collection of Tibetan classics and its inclusive treatment of Buddhist canons of various sects. With a history of over 270 years, the Dêgê Parkhang houses more than 830 ancient books representing the majority of Tibetan classics which are valuable for studies in Tibetan history, politics, economy, religions, and medicine. The Dêgê Parkhang has a collection of more than 300,000 printing blocks. The original printing

methods using manually carved blocks continue to be used here to print the Buddhist Tripitaka canon including *the Ganggyur* and *the Tengyur*. The sutras are beautifully printed with carefully selected materials. Quality control standards are used in each procedure to make sure that the printed pages are clear and durable.

At the Dêgê Parkhang, Dorji's paper is reborn. Each piece of the pliable paper is cut into wide strips which are immersed in water, wrapped in cloth, and then put outside to dry. Nowadays, the use of Tibetan paper is essential to the equally ancient Tibetan art of woodblock printing.

Early next morning, the paper that has been drying through the night is brought into the courtyard as soon as the Dêgê Parkhang is open. The encounter between paper and woodblocks is soon to take place.

Colorful inks are applied to the blocks and pieces of finely-cut paper are placed against the blocks. As the wheel rolls over the blocks, red sutra texts appear on the pieces of thick paper. What people see here are paper and blocks, but what they feel are the serenity and happiness from within. The acts of pressing and printing are just like dharma practices. Printed paper is manually cut, filed, dyed, and eventually bound into volumes. These pieces of paper will be worshiped henceforth by Buddhist followers.

Tibetan Paper

Some say that the history of Tibet is recorded on Tibetan paper. Tibetan paper is made from spurge and hemp fibers processed with lime and natural alkali. The making of Tibetan paper involves dozens of steps, and the materials and herbs used are also needed for making Tibetan incense, hence the high cost.

Paper is one of China's four ancient inventions. Papermaking in Tibet began with a historical Han-Tibetan marriage which took place 1,300 years ago. According to historical records, the Tang Empire forged an alliance with the ancient Tibetan kingdom of Tubo through a peace-making marriage. Princess Wencheng went to Tubo with large numbers of classical Han books. During the reign of Emperor Gaozong, the Tibetan btsan-po (king) invited to his kingdom a cohort of Tang craftsmen who specialized in wine brewing, papermaking, metallurgy, and textile manufacturing. That was how papermaking began to take root in Tibet. In order to produce enough paper for sutra translation, Tibetan paper makers constantly studied the Han craft of papermaking and used locally available materials to eventually produce the unique Tibetan paper. Over the centuries, Tibetan paper has had enormous and far-reaching influences on the Tibetan civilization.

Spurge root fibers are an important material used in Tibetan papermaking. The spurge is a wild poisonous herb called rijia in the Tibetan language. It is the poison in the spurge that makes Tibetan paper vermin-proof and resistant to rotting. Historically, large amounts of Tibetan paper have been used to write and print Buddhist sutras and official documents because of its toughness, pliability, and durability. In addition, it hardly discolors and doesn't allow ink to seep through. The sutras collected in such holy Buddhist monasteries as the Potala and the Qokang have remained intact over centuries of use and weathering largely because they are written or printed on the unique Tibetan paper.

In May 2006, Tibetan paper making was listed among the first group of China's national non-material cultural legacies. In 2009, the title of "National Non-Material Cultural Heritage Propagator" was conferred upon Shering Dorji.

The sacred lake of Tangra Yongtso | 4,528
Tibet | meters above sea level

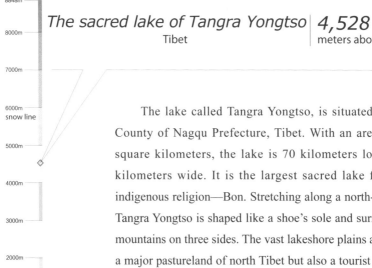

The sacred lake of Tangra Yongtso | 4,528
Tibet | meters above sea level

The lake called Tangra Yongtso, is situated in Nyima County of Nagqu Prefecture, Tibet. With an area of 1,400 square kilometers, the lake is 70 kilometers long and 20 kilometers wide. It is the largest sacred lake for Tibet's indigenous religion—Bon. Stretching along a north-south axis, Tangra Yongtso is shaped like a shoe's sole and surrounded by mountains on three sides. The vast lakeshore plains are not only a major pastureland of north Tibet but also a tourist destination that combines natural beauty with nature preservation.

SPACE FOR IMAGINATION IMPARTED BY THE EARTH: FIELD MASTER DORJI AND HIS SPRING PLOWING FESTIVAL

Crops can hardly grow above the altitude of 4,500 meters. Highland barley, a most hardy plant and the most important grain crop of the farmers, is grown here nevertheless. With more than 70 strains, it is an ancient crop unique to the Qinghai-Tibet plateau.

An old man is worshiping Tangra Yongtso in front of the crystal-clear water. It is the largest sacred lake of the ancient Bonpo religion, and it is said to be the heart of the ancient Zhang Zhung Kingdom of more than one thousand years ago. The altitude here is more than 4,500 meters, but a warm humid microclimate prevails on the lake and in its nearby mountains. A few hundred patches of farmland lie across a small strip of land near the sacred lake. These patches of land are small, but each has a name of its own, like "the fox tail" or "the place where the moon rises." This tells how they are cherished by their owners.

The land is so precious that everything about farming must be considered carefully. The special position of the field master has thus come into being. Field Master Dorji's father was also a field master, and so was his grandfather.

One early morning, Dorji comes to an old house in the village. His fingers move carefully on the wall in search of a special spot. He leans against this spot and looks toward the rising sun on top of the mountain in order to find another spot.

Dorji does calculations according to the ancient calendar and then decides on an important date. What the field master needs most is water. Close to the Tangra Yongtso as they are, the farmers cannot use the water for irrigation not only because the water is salty but also because it is the sacred lake. Water for the entire village comes exclusively from the melting snow in the mountains.

The Spring Plowing Festival is a grand festival in Dorji's village when people pray and hold celebrations before plowing and sowing. People get up this morning and put on their best clothes for the festival. The families bring together the highland barley liquor they have saved. People get together at the irrigation reservoir where Dorji talks about what they did last year and what they plan to do this year.

"We have 260 mu of land to irrigate," says Dorji. "We've got to do it step by step."

When his report is done, people mix water with fermented barley and splash it into the sky, after which the carnival begins. People eat and drink and compete against each other to see who can place the heaviest stone in the center of the reservoir. They build a column of big stones and tie hatas to it. They sprinkle tsampa over the field master to pray for a prosperous year. Children also join in the carnival by playing to their heart's content and splashing the clear water that is running through the irrigation channels.

On the second day of the Spring Plowing Festival, rituals continue to be held near the water-filled reservoir. Water is released from the reservoir after the festival, and now the seeds will return to earth. The earth gives man endless room for imagination, even in the narrow space between towering mountains.

KIND THOUGHTS ARE THE BEST COMPANY: THE EIGHTY-YEAR-OLD TWIN SISTERS

    The celebrations are still going on in Dorji's village, but 80-year-old Tsomo is dozing off. She's already gone to visit her twin sister in her dream.

    Tsomo's sister is named Wangmo, the one she cares about most. Wangmo is a devout dharma practitioner. She has been back to her home village only once since she came to Tangra Yongtso 20 years ago to begin her dharma practice in a hermitage. Wangmo lives in a small room on the hill. Old as she is, Wangmo circumambulates the holy hill beside the lake every day, although she has to walk with great effort on her weak legs.

It has been six months since the sisters met last time. Tsomo is worried that her sister has not been well lately. She gets up early in the morning, prepares many delicacies including fried dough, and then sets out to visit her sister.

"How are you?" Tsomo asks her sister.

"Come here!" says Wangmo.

Wangmo sees the cameraman and asks her sister: "Are they playing a movie?"

"No, they are shooting one," says Tsomo. "Then they will broadcast it."

"Why us? There are so many old people around," asks Wangmo.

"Because we are twins, and old," answers Tsomo.

"I see…" murmurs Wangmo.

"We were born together, and we are old and still together."

"My sight is failing. How's yours?"

"I can't see the sheep clearly from the hill."

"I am worried because it is hard for me to see the characters in the news on TV. But I'm also thinking that it's time to take care of my heart rather than my body at this age. Now, try this. How's it?"

"Let's share."

"I'm not eating. These are too hard for my teeth. How does it taste? Good?"

"Yummy. It tastes so good with sugar."

The sisters take a walk along the lakeshore, and there is so much to talk about. They are both satisfied with their life. Wangmo is already used to her peaceful life. "Kind thoughts are the best companion," says Wangmo to her sister. "Only in the company of kind thoughts is one free from care and confusion."

Highland Barley

Highland barley is a cereal grain of the genus Hordeum in the family Poaceae. It is also named hulless (or "naked") barley, yuanmai, or midamai because its inner and outer glumes are separate. It can be subdivided into a few strains based on their white, black, or dark-green colors. It is mostly grown in Tibet, Qinghai, Sichuan, and Yunnan. As the Tibetan people's staple food, highland barley represents more than half of Tibet's harvest or even more than 80% of the harvest in some cold highland areas. There is such a long history of highland barley cultivation on the Qinghai-Tibet Plateau that this crop has come to embody the unique highland ethnic culture.

Highland barley is popular among the Tibetans as their staple food. It is eulogized in folk songs and stories and the guozhuang circle dance. Vivid accounts are also given of the legendary origin of highland barley; of how it is sowed, tended, harvested, and threshed; and of how the highland barley flour is made and barley liquor brewed. There are many myths, stories, and songs about the origin of highland barley, and most of them tell of dogs, birds, or cranes bringing barley seeds to people. "The Origin of Highland Barley Seeds", one such typical story, is collected in *the History of Tibetan Literature*. The story goes that a prince named A Chu steals highland barley seeds from the snake king who catches and transforms him into a dog. The daughter of a local chieftain falls in love with him and thus turns him back into a human being. The couple then begins to grow highland barley. Through their hard labor, they eventually get to taste aromatic barley liquor and fragrant tsampa, the highland barley flour milled from golden barley grains. After each harvest the first tsampa dough is offered to the dog in appreciation of its bringing the barley seeds to the farmers.

Highland barley is highly nutritious with prominent medical and health-promoting benefits. It is used to brew barley liquor and make tsampa dough.

Tsampa is the Tibetan people's traditional staple food. Tsampa is a Tibetan word meaning "fried flour." The making of tsampa dough is simple. The first step is to roast and mill sun-dried barley grains. Then melt a piece of ghee in a cup of hot milk tea, and put in an adequate amount of the flour. Finger-stir the mixture until the tsampa dough is ready to eat. Meat and wild herbs are also mixed in the tea sometimes to make a porridge called tuba. The tsampa dough fits in well with the nomadic lifestyle because it is easy to prepare and carry. Tibetan herdsmen usually carry tsampa in cloth or leather bags when they travel long distances. They also bring along ghee, tea leaves, salt, and wood bowls so that they can have a meal of tsampa whenever hot water is available.

The highland barley is more nutritious than rice, corn, and wheat. A traditional food on the Tibetan table, now tsampa is also served in Tibetan restaurants in Lhasa. Tibetan people sprinkle tsampa on religious holidays to express good wishes.

The Spring Plowing Festival

Spring means life and hope for people everywhere across the world. After the New Year, things wake up from their winter sleep, and that marks the restart of the farming cycle. The Tibetan Spring Plowing Festival is such a spring holiday.

The Spring Plowing Festival is the time when people celebrate sowing and plowing in spring. After the date of lichun, the Han people's solar term literally meaning "spring begins," snow melts and the earth warms up after the cold winter months. As the most important day in spring, the festival does not have a fixed date. Calculations are needed to decide when to celebrate it based on the Tibetan solar terms and local climates. The festival falls approximately on the date of yushui, the Han people's solar term meaning "rain water." Experienced farmers usually choose to start sowing and plowing on or around the day of yushui when the weather is optimal.

On this day, religious men and women from Tibet's farming areas are fully dressed up for the festival. They come on dancing steps to the barley fields with snow-white hatas and home-brewed barley liquor. They toss tsampa into the sky to pray for seasonable weather and a good harvest. Then they soon begin plowing and sowing after the ritual. After a day's work, the villagers, old and young, get together to drink and dance. The festivities are as joyous as those of the New Year.

The Spring Plowing Festival indicates the social development of the highland. It represents the Tibetan people's wishes for happiness and good harvests.

Religions in Tibet

Most Tibetans believe in Buddhism, Bon, or folk religions and a small number of them believe in Islam and Christianity. In the Tibetan Autonomous Region, there are currently over 1,700 Tibetan Buddhist monasteries with more than 40 thousand monks and nuns, over 80 Bon temples with more than 3,000 monks and 130 thousand followers, 4 mosques with more than 3,000 Muslims, and 1 Christian church with more than 700 Christians.

These religions have varied influences on different social groups and in different geographical areas. Unlike Tibetan Buddhism, Bon, Islam and Christianity, the folk religions have no clergies, theologies, or fixed religious venues. In terms of their interactions, Tibetan Buddhism and Bon have been mutually confrontational yet assimilative in history, and both have assimilated much from Tibet's folk religions. Islam and Christianity only have limited influences in certain geographical areas because of the small number of their followers. Generally speaking, they both exist in harmony with the predominant religions of Tibetan Buddhism and Bon.

Tibet's supposed status as a Buddhist society was in fact an anomaly that resulted from the unification of politics and religion in old times. People had no physical freedom, let alone religious freedom. In the process of Tibet's democratic reform, the upper clergy's prerogatives as well as their exploitative systems were abolished along with the feudal serfdom in order to ensure the lower clergy and general public's right to religious freedom. Monks and nuns who chose to remain in their monasteries and convents had their living conditions taken care of. After the democratic reform was completed, physical and religious freedom became a reality for the low clergy and general public. Nowadays, Buddhist followers hang prayer flags and build mani cairns everywhere in Tibet. Some well-known monasteries are filled with pilgrims and practitioners of circumambulation and prostration. Wedding and funeral customs with religious associations are fully respected. Practitioners are free to have scripture halls and shrines in their homes. They can take pilgrimage trips to monasteries and sacred lakes and mountains. They can also participate in other religious rituals and activities ranging from circumambulation to presenting offerings and chanting sutras.

Bon, Tibet's Primitive Religion

Bon, or the Bonpo religion, is one of the most ancient religions in the world. Bon was prevalent in the ancient Kingdoms of Tubo and Zhang Zhung before Buddhism was introduced into China. It had great influences on the ethnic cultures of Tibet and its neighboring regions with its enormous hoard of knowledge in medicine, astronomy, calendar, geography, divination, painting, and philosophy. Bon originated in Zhang Zhung, today's Tibetan prefecture of Ngari.

The Bonpo religion and its traditions are an embodiment of the Tibetan people's culture. Like many other peoples in the world, ancient Tibetans experienced a long process of the development of primitive religions. Ancient inhabitants of Tibet were in awe of mysterious natural changes and the heaven, the earth, the sun, the moon, and the stars. Their reverence for and worship of natural phenomena gradually evolved into religious beliefs, which under the influence of foreign cultures have become the indigenous Bonpo religion with its unique characteristics coming from Tibet's geography and ethnic culture.

In its early stages, Bon featured the worship of heaven, earth, water, fire, and snowy mountains. Later, worshiping of guardian gods and ancestors became central to Bonpo beliefs. Buddhism was introduced into Tibet from India in the 7th century BCE. This was followed by confrontations between Bon and Buddhism. The two religions, however, also learned from each other so that mutual assimilation of their doctrines has brought them closer to each other. While the many Buddhist sects have adopted many Bonpo doctrines and rituals, Bon has also adopted some Buddhist sutras in order to develop its own precepts. Nowadays, Bonpo traditions continue to be followed in some of Tibet's northern and eastern regions.

Tibetan Buddhism

Buddhism was introduced into Tibet from central China, India, and Nepal in the 7th century. In order to take a foothold and flourish in Tibet, Buddhism assimilated many Bonpo doctrines and rituals. Under the influence of the many cultures in Tibet's neighboring regions, Buddhism became a regionally and ethnically characteristic religion with elaborate doctrines, enormous volumes of sutras in Tibetan, well-structured hierarchies of the clergy, a strict educational system of sutra learning, well-defined dharma practice steps, and unique living Buddha reincarnation systems. Over the years, it has developed into what is known as Tibetan Buddhism, or Lamaism, as distinct from Han Buddhism (based on scriptures in Chinese) and Theravada Buddhism (based on scriptures in Pali).

Tibetan Buddhism has developed into many schools and sects, and many of them have had extensive and important influences on China's history as well as the Tibetan culture and society. The major Tibetan Buddhist schools include Nyingmapa (commonly "the Red Sect"), Sakyapa (commonly "the Multicolored Sect"), Kagyupa (commonly "the White Sect"), and Gelugpa (commonly "the Yellow Sect"). The Gelugpa with a comparatively shorter history has become a dominant school that adopts the living Buddha reincarnation systems using the titles of the Dalai Lama and the Panchen Lama.

Tibetan Buddhist parishes are mostly found in Tibet and the Tibetan prefectures in Qinghai, Gansu, Sichuan, and Yunnan, as well as regions where the Mongolian, Tu, Yugu, and Menba ethnic groups live in compact communities. Small numbers of Tibetan Buddhists are also found in the ethnic groups of Han, Naxi, Luoba, and Pumi. Historically, Tibetan Buddhism was introduced into Bhutan, Nepal, Mongolia, Kashmir, and Russia's Buryatia and Kalmyk republics. Tibetan Buddhism was introduced into Europe and the United States in the second half of the 20th century.

DRINKING AND GETTING DRUNK TOGETHER FOR THE CHICKEN FEET MILLET HARVEST

It's been four months since the honey collection in Chentang, Tibet when the people fulfilled their mission of obtaining beeswax for Buddha statue making. People are now getting busy for the upcoming harvest.

The staple food crop here is chicken feet millet which is mostly reaped by women. Basket on back and curved knife in hand, these women are cutting rice ears skillfully. The rice ears are spread on the ground to be sun-dried and then the rice grains are extracted by pounding.

This chicken-foot-shaped grain contains special life-enhancing nutrients. Requiring round-the-year effort to cultivate, much of the rice harvested is used by the women to brew liquor. The liquor is mixed with hot water and drunk through a straw. It is the men's favorite beverage.

When the harvest is almost completed, one of the families in the village has finished building a new house. Amidst cheers, a patriarch hangs corn and a hata on the beam of the new house, and the carnival begins.

The chicken feet millet liquor is the most important part of the carnival. Men with braided hair drink the liquor and start singing and dancing. They derive no end of enjoyment from these songs and dances, which come from within their hearts. The 92-year-old granny is also drinking with relish. People put quite a few straws in the bucket; they drink and get drunk together. The carnival will last three days and three nights.

When the reaping is done, people will take a one-day walk deep into a forest to arrive at a cluster of mysterious hot springs. Here are 9 natural hot springs in which the farm workers will refresh themselves from their year-long labor. There is a secret belief that has been handed down from generation to generation: disrespect for the springs will turn them cold. This is the interior of the "Third Pole", where people live, work, and receive gifts from the earth.

Chicken Feet Millet and Rice Liquor

Chicken feet millet, also called "dragon-claw rice" or "African rice", is a drought-resistant cereal grain of the genus Gramineae. Its crooked spikes are shaped like chicken feet, hence its name.

Chicken feet millet is an indigenous grain of Africa with a long history of cultivation. In Tibet, it is grown in warm and humid areas below the altitude of 2,500 meters such as the counties of Mêdog, Zayü, and Nyingchi.

Chicken feet millet is the staple food for Sherpa, Menba, and Luoba peoples. They eat it and traditionally use it to brew liquor. The many ethnic groups use more or less the same techniques to brew the chicken feet millet liquor. The rice is cooked and then cooled down to a certain temperature. The cooled rice is mixed with yeast and sealed in specially made jars for fermentation. The jars will be buried underground for a few days.

Though people use similar brewing procedures, the ways they drink the liquor vary widely. The Menba and Luoba people put the fermented rice into a bamboo stalk with a plug on the bottom. They pour water into this container and remove the plug to allow the liquor to fill their drinking utensils. Sherpas from Chentang, however, drink the liquor with straws. They put straws in the fermented rice in a bucket. Then they pour in some warm water and stir the mixture, and the liquor is ready. They keep drinking until the liquor becomes virtually tasteless, and then they will replace what is left with a new "pulp." A bucket of liquor like this can be enjoyed by one person alone or by three to five people who chat as they sip.

The chicken feet liquor is tied inextricably to the Sherpa people's sentiments; it bears witness to life's important occasions. A woman after labor drinks the liquor because it is said to help with lactation; after a day's work, a man refreshes himself by drinking a bucketful of it. A bucket of such liquor is presented as a gift when a baby is born or when someone passes away. Such a present is also appropriately used as a token of appreciation for a favor.

The Chentang chicken feet millet liquor does not have high alcohol content, but its strength is felt gradually. The warm aromatic liquor with its sour, sweet, and bitter tastes are savored in the mouth and allowed to diffuse slowly into one's blood. Like the temperament of the Sherpa people, the liquor is moderate but charmingly bold and outright. Today, the Chentang chicken feet millet liquor has been listed as one of China's national non-material cultural heritages.

Chanang County | 3,680
Tibet | meters above sea level

Chanang County | 3,680
Tibet | meters above sea level

8848m
8000m
7000m
6000m
snow line
5000m
4000m
3000m
2000m
1000m
500m
200m
0m

Under the jurisdiction of Tibet's Lhoka Prefecture, Chanang County is located on the middle reach of the Yarlung Zangbo in south-central Tibet. It is divided by the Yarlung Zangbo River into a southern and a northern part which are roughly the same size. Chanang County has high mountains on the north and the south and valley plains on both banks of the river. It is a county with numerous cultural relics, historical sites and inhabited landscapes. The river banks of the Yarlung Zangbo River are ideal tourist resorts as well as the holy land for Buddhist pilgrims. Chanang in Tibetan means "the interior of thorn-tree-grown ravines and prunus forests."

SONAM THE HIGHLAND SAND CONTROL WORKER WHO TURNS THE DUNES INTO BEAUTIFUL LANDSCAPES

There is an expanse of sand dunes in Lhoka on the middle reach of the Yarlung Zangbo River. These dunes are formed as a result of the seasonal changes of the Yarlung Zangbo River's water level. When the water is low in winter, the river bed is exposed so the cold highland wind blows the sand onto the low land on the riverbanks to form these sand dunes.

Sonam, a desert-control worker, walks through these dunes every day. A group of tree growers are always seen amid the sandy winds. Their mood livens up when the wind stops. This is a gigantic national project: there's no winning the war against desertification with one battle.

"To grow trees here, water is the primary problem to be solved," says Sonam. "So we must dig wells in the first place and then bury water pipes and install sprayers." It is not difficult to get water from beneath the dunes, but the water pipes are often sand-blocked so the water cannot be pumped to farther dunes.

Fortunately, there are many ways to control the desert. They encircle the dunes with poplar and willow trees and then divide the dunes into patches with rows of small wood sticks. Shrub seeds are planted in these small patches. The workers are changing these dunes into a picture under the scorching sun.

Once in a while, Sonam will visit the trees he planted as a young man and listen to their whispers. Sonam has lost count of the trees he has planted in the past three decades. He believes that this valley will change into a forest someday.

BORN HAPPY: HIGHLANDERS POUNDING THE AGA

Workers moving to loud and joyful singing—this is a unique scene of Tibet. The aga clay, a special construction material, is found on the plateau. The process of gradually compacting a mixture of gravel and the clay to form a roof or a floor is called "pounding the aga."

Aga pounding is a collaborative task done by a group of people. People of older ages work in a group and gradually pound the gravel and clay into a solid layer. When the clay is mixed with water, sustained enthusiasm is now needed to keep pounding. This is a seemingly endless process in which a small piece of ground is pounded for 7 to 8 days. The aga is constantly dried, watered, and pounded. A roof made with the aga clay is so tough and durable that it will never cave in even if the supporting beams collapse underneath.

A group of young people pounding the aga contribute a modern look to the ancient work site. They are dressed variously: some young lads are in sports suits and some young girls in Tibetan costumes. Their singing voices are as joyful as their clanking blows are rhythmic. Pounding the aga, people change into pleasant work what would otherwise be drudgery. The highlanders are a happy people by nature.

In pounding the aga, what is sung is not as important as the free movements of arms and legs and the heartfelt happiness. The Tibetans say that the aga is not stones, nor clay, but the essence of the earth.

Aga Pounding

Aga pounding is a traditional Tibetan architectural technique used to build the roof and the floor of a house. A unique type of clay called aga is mixed with gravels and water to make a mixture that is spread on the ground or the roof. After repeated manual pounding, it will become solid, smooth, and water-proof.

Bricks and tiles were the major building materials used in central China before the invention of cement and concrete. Yet it is extremely difficult to manufacture bricks and tiles on the Qinghai-Tibet Plateau because the air is thin. That's why aga clay has been used as a major construction material for Tibetan construction since ancient times. And this technique has been handed down to this day.

The Tibetan word aga means "white matter," a powder produced from weathered lime rocks or other rocks with a predominant content of calcium carbonate. The aga is usually used to build roofs and floors. Aga pounding is a multi-step process. Pieces of the aga clay are pounded into small grains. These are pounded with a specially made tool following an order in which rougher grains are pounded first and finer ones pounded later. Water is sprinkled onto

the aga while it is being pounded until it shows a flat and shiny surface. Then, natural glues and fat are applied to the surface to increase its water-resistance. As part of its daily maintenance, it will be rubbed with ghee and lambskin to keep its surface smooth and shiny. Roofs and floors built with aga look like marble: they are not only flat and smooth but also hard and durable.

In history, the Tibetan people have formed the habit of working to their songs. Working is always accompanied by singing: farmers are singing while sowing seeds and reaping crops; herdsmen are singing while herding the cattle and making ghee. Aga pounding is no exception. It is a collaborative job requiring coordinated movements of a group of people. Singing can make the hard and mechanical labor enjoyable; it promotes efficiency while maintaining fine physical and mental states on the part of the workers. What people sing when they pound the aga are mostly folk songs like the chanteys, or work songs, sung by laborers in central China. It's quite a spectacle to see these people standing in two rows and working to the rhythm of their songs with synchronized movements of their hands and feet. Today, aga pounding is not only a traditional technology but also a unique part of Tibet's folklore.

The
ཨོཾ་འཛམ་གླིང་ **Third**
ཡངས་ཆེ།། **Pole**

ONE SHOULD BE AWARE OF OTHER
PEOPLE'S NEEDS. BE CHARITABLE
WITH PEOPLE IN NEED, FOR GOOD
KARMA WILL BRING ITS RETRIBUTION.

THE HIGHLAND SONGS

Compared with the North and the South Poles, the "Third Pole" is richer in color. The plateau is beautifully decorated with continuous mountain ranges, towering snowy mountains, and peaceful lakes. Large pasture grounds stretch across valleys and on gentle slopes. In their singing, the herdsmen never tire of praising the "Third Pole," their lovely and colorful homeland.

Amdo
Tibet
4,800
meters above sea level

The Amdo Grassland is one of the four great grasslands in northern Tibet. It is larger than the other three put together. The annual Horse Race Festival is an important holiday for the Amdo herdsmen. Many days before the festival, people from all quarters arrive here, pitch their tents, and get ready for the celebrations. In the past, the herdsmen had to travel long, tiring distances on horseback. With increased income, however, these men have bought their own vehicles in recent years, mostly pickup trucks which they use to carry their horses, tents, and family members.

MEN AND HORSES ARE EQUAL: DORJI AND SHIDZI

Two camping zones form naturally: one for carnival and the other the horseraces. The horses are led to the riverside and driven into the river. This is an ancient way of horse training. It is said that the cold water can help regulate the horse's vital energy. The master of a horse will decide on how long his horse should stay in the river based on his estimation of how much energy the horse has just used in a race.

Tsering Targye comes again with his old horse. His son Dorji follows him quietly and sits down in silence.

Tsering Targye knows that Dorji loves horses, especially this old horse named Shidzi. Twelve-year old Shidzi has won five championships. Shidzi is known to everyone who has participated in the races. Once he got a hoof injured in a race, but he won the championship nevertheless.

Dorji braids Shidzi's tail in a new style each day. It is evident to everyone that Dorji has come with a strong wish to win the championship with his horse.

The jockeys are mostly children aged between 7 and 10 years old because of their advantages in body weight. Good performance, however, also depends on skillful horsemanship.

The father knows that his son should face reality.

"Dad," Dorji asks uncertainly. "Can I run the race tomorrow?"

"The way you ride the horse is not quite right," says Tsering Targye patiently and soothingly. "You should not hold the reign this way when running the 'great race.'" You certainly have no problem riding an ordinary horse, but you are not yet able to handle the best horses. Your younger brother Tsering Chönyi is the better jockey. He is smaller than you; he was running the race at age six. He's really better in horsemanship. Be a good boy!"

Hearing these words, Dorji buries his tearful face in his robe and sobs silently. Tsering Targye gently strokes Dorji's head to sooth him. It begins to rain, but no one stops the training because the race is soon to begin.

The race begins. So does the seven-day carnival with bright-colored tents, strong horses, and people in their best attire. Yet Tsering Targye and his family members, who have been preparing for the race, are unexpectedly silent.

In their tent, the Tsering Targye says to his son: "You must care for the horses. For us Tibetans, especially for us horsemen of the grassland, men and horses are equal."

"Dad, is our horse gonna win the race tomorrow?"

"That's hard to say. There are going to be two hundred horses running the race. Winning the race is no easy job."

By early next morning, Dorji's younger brother Tsering Chönyi has arrived. As father's chosen jockey, he is still very young. Their relatives say that Tsering Chönyi has the manner of a skillful master on horseback; from birth he was an equestrian prodigy."

The race is about to begin, yet Tsering Targye has made a decision at the last moment to have Tsering Chönyi run the race on one of the family's other horses. Old Shidzi will be ridden in the race by a relative's son.

The father tells his son: "Be careful! That's the most important thing. Take control of the horse. Don't bump into others: you are not riding alone."

The eight-kilometer race, or the "great race," will begin soon. People are crowding around the race field. Not only are they dressed in fine attire, but also their horses are decked out with elaborate trappings. Dorji is not running the race, but he leads Shidzi to the race field.

At the moment the race starts, a compelling sense of mission takes hold of the young jockeys. More than 200 racehorses reach full gallop, but many fall behind even before they get the chance to gain speed. People are shouting at the top of their voices to cheer the young jockeys and racehorses. One by one, the horses dash across the finish line amidst loud cheers.

Shidzi takes the fifth place, which is not bad, but deep inside Dorji believes that the jockey should have done better. Many hatas are presented to Shidzi and Dorji. Dorji feels like a hero leading his beloved horse.

Tsering Chönyi fails to take even the third place with his new horse, but he is not dispirited for he is only a seven-year-old boy. Now he is looking forward to next year's and is strongly motivated to win the championship.

People are going home after the carnival. Tsering Targye and his sons are also packing their tent and horse gear. The father and sons are sitting on the ground and Tsering Targye lovingly touches his sons on the head. His kids have grown up a little bit at the close of the festival.

The Horserace Festival

Horses have long been close companions to the Tibetan people, so there are many Tibetan holidays associated with the horse. These are horserace festivals in various forms across Tibet. Across the vast territory of Tibet, many horseracing events, combined with a range of other activities, are held as seasonal festivals.

The Tibetan people have an innate affection for horses, and horseracing is an integral part of their recreational activities. A horserace means a leisurely gathering for farmers and herdsmen; it is the opportunity for an exchange of experiences in agriculture and husbandry. In particular, it gives expression to the Tibetan people's pastoral ethos. With their special fondness for horses, the Tibetan people have created an ethnically unique horseracing culture. They celebrate a range of horserace festivals such as the North Tibet Horserace Festival, the Gyangzê Darma Festival, and other such festivals in the cities and counties of Kangding, Panpo, Bairi Poi Ranggyong, Damxung, and Tingri.

The Gyangzê Darma Festival is a traditional holiday celebrated by the local people of Shigatse. The Tibetan word darma means horseback archery. Originally, this festival with a history of 600 years was not all about horseracing. It was initially observed to commemorate a Gyangzê dharma prince and his much respected grandfather. The dharma prince Rabten Kunzang Phak was remembered for the Palcho Monastery and the Kumbum stupa he built. The many religious activities of the festival were gradually replaced by horseracing, a tradition which later became popular in Lhasa, Changtang, and Gongbo. The festival used to be celebrated around April 19th of the Tibetan calendar, and the festivities included horseracing, archery, and wrestling, as well as the unrolling of a huge Buddha painting, shamanic dance, and sacrificial offerings. Today, the festival is mostly celebrated in the slack season in June. The city of Gyangzê is full of joyful and noisy celebrations during the festival.

The North Tibet Horserace Festival is a grand traditional festival of the northern Tibetan grassland held in June of the Tibetan calendar. Lasting from 5 to 15 days, the festival is known as Daqiong in the Tibetan language and also called Yaji because it is held in summer. Compared with Gyangzê, the vast grassland of North Tibet provides a more suitable venue for horseracing. A few days before the festival, herdsmen in their best attire come together from across North Tibet. They will swarm toward the horseracing field bearing highland barley wine, yoghurt, and dried meat, and they pitch beautiful tents around the field.

Besides the traditional events of horseracing, archery, and horsemanship, other activities like weight-lifting, tug-of-war, and the King Gesar epic singing are also featured. Trade fairs are also part of the festivities.

Grassland horseraces include such events as long race, short race, archery on horseback, and horsemanship. Long races include the great race, minor race, and trotting. The jockeys are mostly ten-year-old boys. Before the race begins, highly respected and prestigious lamas grant empowerments for all the jockeys. Upon hearing the starter's gun, scores of horses dash toward the finish line like thunderbolts as thousands of grandly attired spectators cheer the jockeys. The champion of the race usually receives a horse or an equivalent sum as reward. The highest reward however, certainly lies in the honor of the championship. Hatas of good wishes will be presented to the winner, and folks from the same tribe or pasturage area will lead his horse in a jubilant parade. The jockey and his horse will soon become known across his pasturage zone and he will be treated as an honored guest wherever he goes.

Trade fairs are often held during the horserace festivals. The herdsmen sell their products such as ghee and lake salt; they also buy daily necessities and production tools.

Doilung Dêqên County 4,300
Tibet
meters above sea level

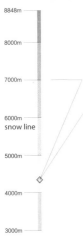

8848m
8000m

7000m

6000m
snow line

5000m

4000m

3000m

2000m

1000m

500m
200m
0m

Doilung Dêqên County | 4,300
Tibet | meters above sea level

Under the jurisdiction of Lhasa, Doilung Dêqên County is 12 kilometers from downtown Lhasa. It is located on the bend of the Lhasa River and its branch Doilong River at the middle reach of the Yarlung Zangbo in south-central Tibet. Doilung Dêqên has agriculture as its major industry, with equal importance attached to animal husbandry. Doilung means "the upper valley" in the Tibetan language and "bliss" in the Dêqên dialect.

THE SACRED PRAYER FLAGPOLE AND THE SAGA DAWA FESTIVAL

On the Qinghai-Tibet Plateau, another holiday called the Saga Dawa Festival is celebrated. People come from all corners to worship a prayer flagpole.

Twenty-nine meters long, the pole weighs 2.3 tons. It is fully covered with yak hide and five-colored prayer flags. Ten thousand people sit in front of the monastery in devout anticipation of the erection of the pole. Following the instructions, the monks are pulling a rope. To a fanfare of sonorous trumpets, people position near the pole and help to plant it by filling in stones at its base. Meanwhile practitioners lean their foreheads against the pole and pray devoutly.

The Saga Dawa Festival

The Saga Dawa Festival falls on April 15th of the Tibetan calendar. According to the Tibetan calendar, April is called Saga Dawa, the month in which Saga (one of the 28 prominent stars in Tibetan almanac) appears, so it is also called the month of Saga. In Tibetan Buddhist traditions, this month is closely associated with Buddha Sakyamuni's dharma mission, and Saga Dawa has thus assumed religious implications. Accordingly, people engage in various commemorative activities during this month. Tibetan Buddhist practitioners chant sutras, practice prostration, ban cattle slaughtering, and accumulate merits and virtues. A range of Buddhist rituals will be held in large and small monasteries.

April 15th is celebrated as the anniversary of Buddha Sakyamuni's birth, awakening, and nirvana. This is when the performance of Buddhist rituals and charitable deeds reaches its peak. Each circumambulation path is fully crowded with people forming circles that turn clockwise ceaselessly. Twirling the mani wheel in one hand and fingering a rosary in the other, the practitioners chant mantras, burn juniper incense, and sprinkle tsampa and highland barley wine. Wreathing columns of juniper smoke create a Buddhist atmosphere that permeates each monastery and each corner of Tibet. Devout Buddhist followers commemorate the sacred Buddha Sakyamuni by circumambulation, burning incense, eating Buddhist vegetarian meals, and freeing captive animals.

Dana, or giving alms, has been a tradition during Saga Dawa, whereby the rich give financial help to the poor. It is an act of great merit to free captive animals on this auspicious day, and large groups of people gather near Lhasa Lake to do this good deed.

The Prayer Flags

Prayer flags in five colors are seen fluttering everywhere in sacred places like mountain tops, mountain passes, riverbanks, and Buddhist monasteries. These prayer flags are called lungta, or literally "wind-horse flags", with lung meaning "wind" and ta "horse." The name wind-horse indicates the belief that wind works like a formless horse to carry everywhere the sutras and mantras printed on the flags. People passing by prayer flag sites will often dismount to pray.

These flags are printed with Buddhist mantras and short sutras. Tibetan Buddhists believe that each flap of the flag means the mantras are read once, so the flying flags are communicating their wishes for Buddha's blessings. These flags serve as a bond between people and Buddhist deities; they are a sign of the presence of Buddhist deities and people's wishes.

Prayer flags vary in sizes and are printed with images of Buddha, auspicious symbols, and mantras and sutras in Tibetan. These colored flags are usually hung vertically from prayer poles in squares or in front of monasteries. Small prayer flags printed with images of Buddha and auspicious animals are blue, white, red, green, or yellow in color. They are often strung on long lines and hung in diagonal arrays at sparsely populated mountain passes. Prayer flags hanging on a roof are called "star-flame wordless flags" which comprise a main flag with monochrome edging on four sides and five long flags respectively colored blue, white, red, green, and yellow.

The colors of these flags have differently meanings. It is generally believed that blue stands for sky, white for cloud, red for fire, green for water, and yellow for earth. The order of these flags is fixed, corresponding to the unchanging order of nature with the blue sky above and the yellow earth beneath. The main flag and its edging may appear in one of these five colors but the color of the edging is definitely different from that of the flag itself. This flag is usually hung on the roof as a special symbol of the family living in that house. The color of the main flag represents the birth year of the most respected senior family member. The color white stands for the year of iron, yellow for earth, green for wood, red for fire, and blue for river. The color of the flag's edging cannot be used randomly; it must conform to theory in the Tibetan almanac about the generative or overcoming interactions between mother and son. At the New Year, all the families replace their old mantra flags at about the same time. Mantra flags are also hung on such important occasions as religious holidays, ancestor commemoration, house moving, weddings and even when one takes a pilgrimage or business trip.

Wind-horses flap in the wind, as if chanting the mantras and sutras printed on them. That's why people hang these flags on long poles exposed to the wind in monasteries or on squares. Mantra flag replacement rituals are performed on April 15th of the Tibetan calendar, or the Saga Dawa. Such a ritual includes praying, offering sacrifices, removing the old pole, planting the new pole, and mountain circumambulation. When the old pole is put down, Buddhist followers and visitors will rush forward to grab pieces of the used and discolored flags which they believe will ward off misfortunes. Very soon, people will attach new mantra flags, hatas, spices, and offerings on a new pole which will be planted after a grand ceremony.

Pumo Yongtso | 5,010
Tibet | meters above sea level

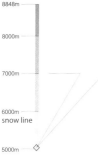

8848m
8000m
7000m
6000m
snow line
5000m
4000m
3000m
2000m
1000m
500m
200m
0m

Pumo Yongtso | 5,010
Tibet | meters above sea level

Located in Nagarzê County, Pumo Yongtso, with an area of 290 square kilometers, is the highest-altitude Tibetan lake. The surrounding snowy mountains, the lake, blue sky, and white clouds make a beautiful landscape painting. The lake is said to have three islands. Lush grasses of the lakeshore are home to an enormous number of wild animals. As one of Tibet's four prestigious *yongtso*, it is a sacred lake believed to have been blessed by the great Buddhist master Padmasambhava.

THE SHEEP OF TUI VILLAGE AND THE HOSPITABLE SACRED LAKE OF PUMO YONGTSO

The altitude of 5,000 meters marks the limit of human activities. Villagers of Tui have been living for generations on pastures at 5,000 meters above sea level. Having once lived on an island of Pumo Yongtso, the villagers later relocated to the lakeshore.

Winter has come and the herbage is getting thinner. More than a thousand sheep are herded against the cold wind to farther pastures.

Food is very scarce in winter and even the pikas are getting worried. They usually eat the grass near their burrows, but now they have to take the risk and go farther for food. This is a good moment for the Tibetan fox to seize its chance. Eating grass away from its burrow, the pika is totally unaware of the impending danger. In a blink of an eye, the pitiful pika turns into a delicious meal for the fox.

There is little grass left after many days of grazing, and only two stretches of pastureland remain on two islands of Pumo Yongtso. The shepherds are waiting for the moment to herd their sheep to these islands.

These are the coldest days at Pumo Yongtso. A warm green color appears at the bottom of the lake, but things look quite different above water, where the ice looks like a gigantic mirror.

It is hard to find pastures nearby. The herding path is extending longer and longer to places more than 10 kilometers away.

"If the weather is bad and windy tomorrow," says one shepherd to another looking at the sheep in the pen, "those pregnant ewes may fall on the ice and get killed. That would be too bad for everyone."

At five o'clock in the morning, people are collecting ashes of burnt cow dung which will be spread on the path leading to the islands. This dung-ash-paved path is very important for keeping pregnant ewes from being injured or killed by falling on the slippery ice. With many ewes being pregnant, anti-skid measures are important for the migrating sheep.

Experience tells these shepherds that they must hit the road before daybreak because strong winds will be blowing on the lake around noontime. That will make it more difficult for the sheep to move forward.

Led by the bellwether, a long line of sheep under the winter sun is moving slowly along the narrow path toward the islands. This is quite a spectacle. Sheep fall on the slippery ice from time to time, so the shepherds hurry over to help them stand up and move forward. Where a sheep cannot stand up, the shepherd will carry it in his arms.

It is hard to say how long it will take the sheep to arrive at the islands. Half a day will be enough in good weather with no wind, the shepherds say, but it may take much longer if it becomes windy.

After trudging a long way the sheep finally arrive at the islands. It is the responsibility of each man from Tui village to take turns shepherding the sheep on the islands. The sheep will be enjoying the lush pasture over the next two weeks.

These men will never let their companions down, no matter how harsh the environment is. For the Tui villagers, the priority is to make it possible for their sheep to live through the winter smoothly.

The first lamb is born. Joyful Migma feeds the lamb with ghee as a nutritious supplement.

More and more lambs are born earlier than anticipated. Ten days have passed and the ice on Pumo Yongtso is melting in large patches. Thinning ice means shortened time at pasture, because the sheep must be moved back to the village before the ice is gone. The cracking of ice deep beneath sounds like constant thunder issuing from black clouds.

The Tibetan New Year is just around the corner. Tui villagers are busy purchasing New Year supplies and it is time for shepherd Mima to return from the island. Mima's mother and wife are busy making a wool carpet to give him a welcome on his return. The women are busy working and hot food is simmering in the pot. Mima's mother sings while working on the carpet: "Here comes the good day for our lad, / Present him wine in a gold bowl. / Here comes the good day for our lad, / Brilliantly shines the gold bowl. / Oh! The Yalong River, / Don't drink it up in one gulp. / This is the good day for our lad…"

On New Year's Day, Tui villagers make a new dung-ash path on Pumo Yongtso for their well-fed sheep to return home. The ice has been melting on both sides of the path. Danger lies in the thinning ice that is supporting a weightier flock. The flock has grown in size because new lives have been born in the past 20 days thanks to the nurturing islands. Tui villagers know that everything has been going smoothly.

Tui villagers are full of hope for the coming year thanks to the islands, new-born lambs, and ice on the lake; they are full of hope thanks to the shepherds' wisdom and skills that have been handed down from generation to generation.

YUGUN'S VULTURE BONE FLUTE

The pastures of Amdo are not a vast stretch of flat land. Rocky hills and mountains rise here and there from the rolling pasturelands. In these mountains live an intriguing species of holy birds—vultures.

Yugun climbs to the top of the cliffs, where he is an unexpected guest. Now in his fifties, Yugun is looking for something to ease his worries. He almost went blind in his left eye last year and had undergone heart surgery the year before last. He is concerned that he has not gotten a chance to pass on his most cherished craft.

The vulture bone flute, made of the vulture's wing bone, has a history of more than 1,000 years. Grassland inhabitants play it to dispel the loneliness they feel while herding their cattle.

Yugun's daughters, both college students in Chengdu, come back home in their summer vacations to help dad with housework. They are talking about their father's vulture bone flutes during a rest break.

"Can you play the vulture bone flute?" the elder sister asks the younger.

"Not quite," she answers.

"It's difficult if you don't know how to move your fingers the right way," says the elder sister. "Dad is getting older."

"That's true," says the younger.

"We have only one vulture bone flute."

Yugun has only one flute for his two daughters. This has been disturbing him as he grows older and his health deteriorates. He decides to make another flute, so he takes a motorcycle trip to visit the herdsmen. "If you find a bone like this," he says to a young herdsman earnestly, "please do me a favor by keeping it for me."

"Sure I will."

"Thank you!"

A herdswoman says to Yugun that she has no idea what kind of bones are needed to make the flute. Yugun tells her that it is the bone in the middle of a vulture's wing.

"I've never seen a dead vulture," says the woman. "But I will call you if I do."

"Can you play a tune on it?" another herdsman asks pointing at Yugun's flute.

"Yes, let me show you." A nice tune is played on the flute.

According to Yugun's father and uncle, a vulture may live ten thousand years old and then soar into the air, higher and higher until it ultimately disappears like rainbow. Though near-sighted, he will never give up; he is determined to hand down the craft of vulture bone flute making. It worries him most that he may die before handing down what he has inherited from his forefathers.

The chances of finding a vulture bone in the vast grassland are slim, but Yugun does not give up. He believes that he will find one. Just when he is on the edge of despair, he is given hope that the long-sought bone will show up soon. A message comes from a herdsman that a vulture bone has been found.

Yugun rushes into the man's courtyard. "Hello! Hello!" he calls out to the man from a distance.

"Hello!" says the host. "Come on in."

"Thanks!"

The herdsman takes out something wrapped in a piece of yellow cloth.

"Pleas show me," says Yugun earnestly.

"Let me open it," says the host unwrapping the cloth.

"Good! It looks nice, but let me check if there's any crack. A crack means the bone is useless," says Yugun with a slight feeling of uncertainty. He checks the bone over and over again.

"Does a crack mean you can't use it?"

"Yes, but you've found a nice bone," says Yugun joyfully.

"I found it a few days ago," says the host smiling.

"Where did you find it?"

"At the top of the Taga Mountain. The vulture died in a fight."

Yugun believes that each vulture bone will come to the craftsman in a mysterious way.

This might be the last vulture bone to come to Yugun in his life. He values it so much that he does not start making the flute right away.

Yugun finally lays out the tools and starts the procedure of measuring, cutting, drilling, and filing. A unique tune eventually comes from inside the bone flute. Grandpa taught his dad how to play the flute and then dad taught him how to play it. Now he will teach his daughters; he is finally able to hand down this tradition. The daughters are happy to have their respective flutes.

Tibetan Vulture Bone Flutes

The vulture bone flute is a unique Tibetan musical instrument made of the longest bone taken from a vulture's wing, hence its name. It is usually played as a solo instrument and is mostly found in Tibet and the Tibetan prefectures in Qinghai, Sichuan, and Gansu.

With a history of more than 1,700 years, the vulture bone flute came into being in nomadic times. Early herdsmen made a primitive version of the flute by simply drilling a few holes in the bone. They played it only for self-entertainment while herding their cattle.

A vulture bone flute is between 24 to 26 centimeters long and 1.5 centimeters in diameter. It is hollow inside with no reeds. Both ends of the flute are open and there are three finger holes on its lower part. To make such a flute, the craftsman saws off the ends, polishes the edges, and removes the marrow. Now there is a larger oval opening on one end and a smaller one on the other. Slightly oval finger holes, each measuring 0.7 centimeters in diameter, are drilled with a 2.2-centimeter interval in between. Strict steps must be followed in drilling the holes. The interval between the finger holes is usually measured with the index and middle fingers placed flat against the bone pipe.

The vulture bone flutes and their end openings vary in size. The intervals between finger holes also vary. After the finger holes are drilled, decorative patterns and inscriptions are carved onto the flute which can now be seen as a piece of artwork.

Vulture bones are extremely difficult to find because of the unique geographical and climatic conditions of Tibet. They are only found in mountains above the altitude of 4,000 meters. It is said that at the last moment of its life, a vulture will fly at the sun until it turns directly into ashes. That's why their bones are rarely found on the ground. The only chance for people to find their bones is when a vulture fails to fly over snow-covered mountains in extreme weather conditions and succumbs to the bitter cold. The ancient lore of the vulture bone flute may become a lost art because of the scarcity of vulture bones.

Axu | 3,680
Sichuan | meters above sea level

8848m
8000m
7000m
6000m
snow line
5000m
4000m
3000m
2000m
1000m
500m
200m
0m

Axu **3,680**
Sichuan   meters above sea level

Axu is a township under the jurisdiction of Dêgê County, Garzê Tibetan Autonomous Prefecture, Sichuan Province. It is 206 kilometers to the northeast of the county of Dêgê. It is said to be the birthplace of Gesar Ling, the protagonist of the Tibetan epic King Gesar. The Axu grassland is a flat plain of beautiful landscapes in the watershed of the Yalong River. Axu is far away from noisy cities. Visitors to Axu are impressed by its fragrant Tibetan barley liquor and pure yak cheese in the way they are touched and enchanted by its simple folk customs.

Epic Singer Sitar Dorji and His Predestined Vocation

Axu is King Gesar's hometown, the place where he was born and raised and where he fought most of the battles in his life. King Gesar (1038-1119) was born to a poor family. He lived with his mother and made a living as a shepherd. At the age of 16, he became King of the Ling Kingdom by winning a horserace. He was a brave and intelligent military strategist who fought all his life to deliver the poor from tyrannical reigns. He unified 150 small and large states to create a strong Kingdom of Ling. He subdued and vanquished demons and oppressors and taught the people agricultural skills. His life story is told in the world's longest epic in the world, which continues to be produced and performed. Today, more than 100 bards from the Qinghai-Tibet Plateau are still chanting the legendary tales of King Gesar.

Sitar Dorji, a special student at Tibet University, is the youngest bard of the epic King Gesar. He is also the only college student among all his fellow bards. Tibet University has launched a long-term filming plan to record his performance.

Sitar Dorji puts on his costumes, walks into the studio, and sits in front of the camera. Now the filming starts.

"The lake resembles holy water, / and the sacred mountain bursts open. /

Who's the one on the throne above the flames / other than Gesar himself? / Norbu Dradul (Gesar) brings together the gods / from hills and ravines, lakes and rivers / to overwhelm the demons and devils / to pray for the spirits of dead ones / to pray for a better afterworld... / King Gesar is meditating in retreat, / so all creatures are exempted from disasters, / and live happily in the Kingdom of Ling, / on the vast grassland where the holy steeds gallop…"

Sitar Dorji with his eyes half-closed seems to have entered an ecstatic trance as he chants. He has been working for four hours this afternoon, but instead of being exhausted, he is delightedly immersed in his chanting.

It will take him more than 100 hours to chant the whole epic he has learned by heart, says Sitar Dorji, and that number is still growing. According to Tibetan traditions, Sitar Dorji became a bard not by learning but through holy inspiration. Most Gesar epic bards are illiterate.

Sitar Dorji works with his professors at the research center to compile Gesar's legend tales on a daily basis. It is amazing that most senior bards in old times, though illiterate, could chant more than a hundred volumes of the Gesar King epic. Sitar Dorji is inheriting and continuing this ancient art. Yet unlike the older bards, he is a college student who plays soccer and basketball with his fellow students. He lives the life of an ordinary college student at school.

"Today, in the Lion-Dragon Palace of the Holy Kingdom, / King Gesar and his thirty soldiers, / seven lieutenant generals and three generals, / distribute among people of the Kingdom of Ling / the treasures of Dagsig Nor Zong, / and pray for them."

This is the song of the highlands. Ancient traditions and modern life converge in this unbroken chant.

The Epic King Gesar

King Gesar is an epic collectively created by the Tibetan people. As a part of Tibet's thousand-year-long oral tradition, it has been compiled into a book of more than 120 volumes. It comprises one million lines or 20 million characters and is the longest epic ever written. Some call it the "Homeric Epic of the East."

King Gesar is believed to be the reincarnation of the great Buddhist master Padmasambhava. The Tibetan people are proud of him as an unparalleled hero, a brave warrior who punishes the evil and protects the good and who spreads Buddhism while propagating cultural traditions. The epic King Gesar came into being at the time while ancient Tibetan tribal society was disintegrating as a slave-holding regime began to take shape. It began to gain popularity in an era when the Tubo Regime collapsed, while the Tibetan society was undergoing tumultuous social changes marking the transition from a slave-holding society to a state of feudal serfdom (the 900s to the early 1100s.)

Drawing from ancient Tibetan myths, legends, poetry, and proverbs, the epic King Gesar represents the peak of ancient Tibetan culture. It gives accounts of fearless and tireless Gesar who fights against heavy odds to overwhelm demons and protect the weak, accomplishing heroic feats for people's benefit. It is a eulogy to just wars that bring peace and justice to the world.

The story begins with the creation of the world when three great Buddhist dharma kings bring forth various miracles. Guru Padmasambhava as the greatest of all dharma kings brings chaotic Tibet under control with his vows. The many demons rebel against him and break loose. Tibet falls apart to become numerous small states ruled by malignant and greedy kings. Tibet is once again under the rule of cannibalistic demons and goblins. To put an end to the chaos, the gods decide to have a hero descend from heaven to overpower the demons. Eventually, the youngest son of Tshangs-pa Dkar-po (Sitabrahma) descends from heaven to be born as a prince of the Kingdom of Ling. He grows up in the blessed land situated between the Yangtze River and the Yalong River in eastern Tibet. He competes against a galaxy of fine horsemen and becomes the respected King Gesar by winning a horserace. King Gesar subdues the cannibalistic demons and vanquishes the invaders, fighting uncompromisingly against the traitors and ultimately restoring peace and happiness to his kingdom. At the age of 80, King Gesar descends to the realm of hell to rescue his wife and mother. In the end, he leaves behind his kingdom on earth and returns to heaven with his wife.

This epic is a literary representation of Tibet's important historical moments and social structures, giving expression to the people's yearnings and ideals while providing an account of how the many ethnic tribes become a cohesive society through constant amalgamation. It is a literary masterpiece that facilitates studies in Tibet's history, society, moral values, ethnic relations and cultures, and folklores and customs.

King Gesar is also an extraordinary literary work: it is the only "living" epic in the world. It continues to be chanted by more than one hundred bards in Tibet, Sichuan, Qinghai, and Inner Mongolia, and the story is still developing.

A King Gesar chanter is called *zhongken* with zhong meaning stories of Gesar and ken a person or bard. As for how many stories a *zhongken* knows and how he has learned them, this remains something of a mystery. This peculiar phenomenon has aroused wide attention.

Those voluble yet illiterate epic chanters are also called *bab sgrung*, "bards as divine instruments." The Tibetan people believe that mastery of the stories and chanting skills comes from gods. It is estimated that there are about 140 King Gesar epic bards among whom many are "divine instruments." Academia has come up with various explanations but no consensus has been reached as to how the divine will actually works.

Mensi | *4,300*
Tibet | meters above sea level

8848m
8000m
7000m
6000m
snow line
5000m
4000m
3000m
2000m
1000m
500m
200m
0m

Mensi | *4,300*
Tibet | meters above sea level

Under the jurisdiction of Gar County of Ngari Prefecture, Mensi Township is located in the Singe Zangbo and Gar Zangbo valleys on the westernmost point of Tibet Autonomous Region. As the center of the first-ever ancient civilization of the Qinghai-Tibet Plateau, it is the birth place of the ancient kingdom of Zhang Zhung.

A Generous Offer: Tsötrim's Tibetan Medicines

Tsötrim is a physician of Tibetan medicine as well as a Buddhist monk in Mensi. As a boy Tsötrim began his dharma practice with his master in this cave and now he has been living here for more than 30 years. It is also in this cave that he concentrates on studying the medical science his master taught him.

Tsötrim uses many electronic devices including an iPhone, a laptop, and a Mac tablet. In this ancient cave, he surfs the internet to find literature for his research. The most important components of the traditional medicines he makes come from various special stones.

Tsötrim takes regular trips to look for stones each year. He picks up stones on the grassland and takes photos of a lake with his tablet. One gets easily lost on the vast grassland of north Tibet, so Tsötrim often has to seek help from local herdsmen. He tells a shepherd that there used to be a path here in his memory. The shepherd draws a map to show him the way. Sometimes a motorist will give him a ride.

This time, Tsötrim finds a magic stone to treat gout. The stones need to be

cooked in water from the sacred lake of Manasarovar. In order to produce authentic Tibetan medicines, Tsötrim goes to great lengths to fetch holy water from Lake Manasarovar.

He breaks the stones into small pieces and cooks them in the holy water with many herbs. Then he grinds the stones into powders. The precious pills he painstakingly makes are mostly given to people in need. He keeps only a small bowl of pills to make offerings to his late master. He will take another trip sometime in the near future.

A deep-seated vow enables Tsötrim to delve into nature and offer his pills in a peaceful state of mind. That wish is a voice issuing from the plateau: receive the sunshine and then bring people fruits.

Tibetan Medicine

Tibetan medicine as a time-honored science has a highly developed system of medical theories and clinical practices. Over the centuries, it has widely assimilated the essentials of Indian, Nepalese, and Sri Lankan medical sciences as well as traditional medicine of the Han Chinese. As a unique branch of traditional Chinese medicine, it has proven effective for the treatment for certain diseases and has contributed to Tibetan people's social development and prosperity.

In their constant efforts to fight diseases, ancient inhabitants of the Qinghai-Tibet Plateau came to understand the medical effects of some herb plants. Meanwhile, ancient hunters also discovered the pharmaceutical values of some animal substances. It is said that a saying came into circulation early in the 3rd century BCE that "medicine exists alongside poison." People also began to use ghee to stop hemorrhaging and lees of highland barley wine to treat wounds. Increased knowledge of nature and agricultural production also contributed to Tibetan people's rich medical knowledge and experience.

According to Tibetan medical theories, the cosmos is composed of the five minor elements of metal, wood, water, fire, and earth and the five major elements of earth, water, fire, wind, and void. While the five minor elements correspond to man's heart, liver, spleen, lungs, and kidneys, the five major elements are essential for the existence of the cosmos. According to the "three functional principles", the human body comprises three humors, namely rlung (wind), mkhris pa (fire), and bad kan (water and earth), and the imbalance among these humors will result in illnesses. Traditional Tibetan medicine has made unique contributions to medical science with its theories of the "three functional principles," "seven major bodily substances," and "three humors."

Tibetan medicine believes that man's health is subject to the influences of environment, climate, and one's daily regimen, and that medical conditions arise as a result of imbalances among the three humors. The causes and nature of a disease are determined through synthetic analyses of general impressions acquired through the diagnostic approaches of inquiry, observation, and auscultation. This shows that traditional Tibetan medicine includes traditional medical theories of the Han Chinese.

The Rrgyud bzhi or Gyushi, known as the Four Tantras, is the major medical book of Tibetan medicine. It was written by the 8th-century Tibetan physician Yuthok Yontan Gonpo and his colleagues. Its rich contents include categorization of illnesses and theories and practices of human physiology, pathology, diagnostics, and pharmaceutics.

In Tibetan medicine, medical conditions show "heat" or "coldness" symptoms and there are medicines for external or internal use. Medicines used internally are based on the principles of "cold medicines for heat symptoms" and "warm medicines for coldness symptoms." Accordingly, Tibetan medicines have either "hot" or "cold" qualities. The use of medication is based on the indicated symptoms as well as the properties and effects of different medicines. External treatments include acupuncture, bloodletting, and cupping. In addition, hot ghee is used to stop bleeding and wine lees are used to treat external wounds. To treat a disease, a Tibetan doctor usually takes into consideration four equally important aspects: diet, daily regimen, internal medicine use, and external treatment.

There are more than 1,400 cures made from numerous pharmaceutical substances, most of which are unique to the Qinghai-Tibet Plateau. Thanks to its unique geography, the Qinghai-Tibet Plateau is home to rich medical resources including more than 1,000 medical herbs representing more than half of the total found in China.

The
༄༅། །འཛམ་གླིང་ Third
ཡར་ཅ།། Pole

EACH CREATURE DESERVES TO BE
RESCUED.

WATER OF BENEVOLENCE

Most of the known civilizations on earth were born near rivers. More than half of the largest rivers in Asia have their headwaters on the Qinghai-Tibet Plateau. The snowy mountains and glaciers provide enough fresh water for more than one billion people living downstream. There are also countless lakes and hot springs here. Life unfolds bountifully thanks to nourishing water.

Burang *3,900*
Tibet | meters above sea level

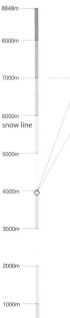

8848m
8000m

7000m

6000m
snow line

5000m

4000m

3000m

2000m

1000m

500m
200m
0m

Burang | **3,900**
Tibet | meters above sea level

As an important land port adjoining Nepal and India on Tibet's southern border, Burang County is located to the south of Ngari. It is a thin strip of land situated on Lake Peacock (Humla Karnali) Valley between the Namuabi and Naimona'nyi (Gurla Mandhata) Peaks in a valley in the southern Himalayas. Humid air currents from Bangladesh create a congenial microclimate here. Burang, "the place surrounded by snowy mountains," has a mild climate and plentiful precipitation. In the north of Burang are the sacred Mountain Kangrinboqê (Mt. Kailash), Naimona'nyi Peak, the sacred lake Mapam Yongtso (Lake Manasarovar), the ghost lake Lhanag Co, and

INDIAN PILGRIMS FROM AFAR

the remains of Korqag and Simbiling Monasteries. These combine to make Burang a well-known Buddhist pilgrimage site and a popular tourist destination.

A group of fatigued yet excited Indians cross the China-Indian border at the Qiangla (Lipulekh) Pass to arrive at Burang. They have travelled from the Gangetic Plains to Burang at 5,000 meters above sea level to accomplish their life-long dreams. They are drawing near their destination, everyone full of excitement.

"The purpose of my trip is to change myself," says a pilgrim. "I come here to see a bit more of the world. The gods lead us here."

These pilgrims stand in the sacred lake Mapam Yongtso and pray devotedly. They hold water in both hands to pay homage to the gods. It is believed that one circumambulatory trip around the lake in the Sheep Year is equivalent to thirteen trips in other years. That's why there are more pilgrims circumambulating the lake in the Sheep Year.

Kangrinboqê in Tibetan means "snow peak of the gods" or "precious jewel of

the snowy mountains." Beliefs in its status as "center of the world" are shared by followers of Bon, Buddhism, Hinduism, and Jainism. It is also the heavenly abode of the supreme Hindu God Shiva.

Kangrinboqê is surrounded by more than 200 glaciers whose water flow into four rivers which are the main headstreams of the Yarlung Zangbo River, the Ganges, and the Indus River. Kangrinboqê, the great god of the snowy mountains, is respected as the source of all rivers.

The sacred lake Mapam Yongtso is believed to be where the gods bathe. One cleans his heart and renews his soul with water from Mapam Yongtso.

These Indian pilgrims hold religious rituals on the lakeside. "I would like this trip to be a present for my husband," says a pilgrim. "We both hope to come back again."

The trip is over with everyone refreshed. Their life-long wishes have been fulfilled.

Sacred Mountains and Lakes

The snowy highland where the Tibetan people live is sparsely populated due to its cold climate. The unpredictable mysteries of nature contributed to the ancient belief that each mountain, river, lake, and forest were inhabited by gods and spirits who ruled the world. All aspects of human society—birth, death, health, fortune, disasters, and harvests—are at the disposal of these holy beings. Worshiping of sacred mountains and lakes thus became a characteristic part of Tibetan people's primitive religious beliefs. This is a tradition inherent in Bon, Tibetan Buddhism, and folk customs. As part of Tibetan people's centuries-old beliefs, worshiping of sacred mountains and lakes gives expression to the people's wishes for peace and harmony as well as the magnanimity of Buddhist philosophy.

There are countless sacred mountains and lakes in Tibet with Kangrinboqê being the most famous sacred mountain and Mapam Yongtso the most respected sacred lake. The two mountains of Kangrinboqê and Naimona'nyi and the two lakes of Mapam Yongtso and Lhanag Co combine to form what is known as "the place of sacred mountains and lakes."

Both Kangrinboqê and Mapam Yongtso are located in Ngari, Tibet. Rising 6,638 meters above sea level, Kangrinboqê is the highest peak of the Gangdisê Mountain Range. Kangrinboqê means "snow peak of the gods" in the Tibetan language and "the heavenly abode of Lord Shiva" in Sanskrit. This is where the Lion River, the Horse River, the Elephant River, and the Peacock River originate, which are the headstreams of the Indus River, the Yarlung Zangbo River (the Brahmaputra River), the Sutlej River (a major tributary of the Indus River), and the Karnali River (a tributary of the Ganges). Being identified with Sumeru, the "central peak of the world" in Buddhist cosmology, it is regarded as the "Sacred Mountain" by Tibetan Buddhists, and it is also regarded as the divine home of Lord Shiva by Hindus. The "Sacred Lake" Mapam Yongtso is located 20 kilometers to the southeast of the "Sacred Mountain." Mapam Yongtso at an elevation of 4,588 meters is the highest freshwater lake and has an area of 412 square kilometers. According to Tibetan historical records, this is also associated with Yaochi (Lake of Immortals) of Goddess Xi Wangmu (Queen Mother of the West) in Han mythology. The "Sacred Mountains and Lakes" is one of the best known tourist destinations of Ngari as well as holy ground for followers of Bon, Buddhism, Hinduism, and Jainism. In recent years, the "Sacred Mountains and Lakes" has been included in the China National Wetland Conservation Action Plan with large annual financial input to preserve the local eco-system. Each summer, pilgrims from India, Nepal, and Tibet swarm here to bathe in the lakes and accumulate merits and virtues.

Markam County | *4,317*
Tibet | meters above sea level

8848m
8000m

7000m

6000m
snow line

5000m

4000m

3000m

2000m

1000m

500m
200m
0m

Markam County | *4,317*
Tibet | meters above sea level

The headwaters of great rivers have provided fitting spaces for evolution of human civilization. In recent years, people all over the world have enthusiastically traced the headwaters of many rivers in order to find out where human cultures originated. The Lancang River, originating in the Dang La Mountain Range, takes a winding course through the Hengduan Mountains.

WORKING WITH NATURE: MARKAM SALT

Markam County is located in southeastern Tibet at the juncture of Sichuan, Yunnan, and Tibet. With Sichuan's Batang County across the river, Markam County borders Yunnan's Dêqên County on the south. On the north and west, it shares borders with the Tibetan counties of Gonjo, Chagyab, and Zogang under the jurisdiction of Qamdo. Since ancient times Markam has been regarded as the southeastern gateway to Tibet and the Ancient Tea Horse Road's first stop in Tibet. Today, the Sichuan-Tibet Highway joins the Yunnan-Tibet Highway here in this county with its simple but distinctive folk customs. Markam is a pristine land blessed with a number of rivers, snowy mountains, and lush virgin forests as well as rich hydrologic, mineral, and forest resources.

Two ethnic groups making a living from the salt industry live on both banks of the Lancang River. The upstream Tibetans are mostly Christians while the Naxi people living downstream are mostly Buddhists. The two groups, though different in religion, have been living in harmony. The two types of salt produced here can be attributed to a shared tradition.

Both banks of the Lancang River here are endowed with springs that contain high salt content. The brine flats are supported by thousands of cedar tree trunks soaked with brine. The secret of salt making lies in the hands of the women.

"I learned salt making from the others," says a salt-making lady. "Mom didn't teach me. I learned it from my sister-in-law. The elders tell us that we have been making salt for more than one thousand years."

Brine flats show different colors because of the earth used to build them. The upstream flats produce white salt and the downstream ones red salt.

Salt is produced through the interactions among sunshine, wind, and water. Salt crystals are shining in the sun. Women bend down to scrape the salt with wooden boards. Here, salt making is a tradition and a pleasant job.

Each brine flat produces salt in three layers—bottom, middle, and upper. Traditionally, the salt is produced by women and sold by men. The salt is bagged and given to horse caravans that carry it on a long journey to the other side of the mountains. This is how man collaborates with nature in a creative way in harsh environment.

A Nyekhong Monastery lama responsible for daily purchases comes back with the salt he has just bought in the market. Food cooked with the brine salt is so palatable that other condiments are rendered unnecessary.

It is not just the monks in this ancient monastery who like the salt. They often spread salt and highland barley grains outside the monastery so that the animals will come from nearby mountains to enjoy their regular breakfast. This place has become home for many wild animals.

The Yanjing Brine Flats

Yanjing, meaning "salt well" in Chinese, is located in south Markam County at the juncture of Tibet, Sichuan, and Yunnan. Situated between the Jinsha River to the east and the Lancang River on the west, Yanjing boasts plentiful natural resources. The name Yanjing comes from its rich salt deposits and brine wells. The Tibetan word for Yanjing is Chakaluo, meaning "the place where salt is produced." Presently, Yanjing has become a nature reserve.

The Yanjing brine flats are unique evidence of human handiwork in the landscape. Yanjing used to be the passageway connecting the Tubo and Nanzhao Kingdoms and the only route for transporting tea from Yunnan to Tibet. These are the only surviving brine flats on the Ancient Tea Horse Road where salt is produced by a traditional artisanal process. In addition, Yanjing is where the only Christian church and parish are found in Tibet. The century-old Yanjing Christian Church is the only functional Catholic building in Tibet. In this ancient town of the Hengduan Mountain Valley, harmonious coexistence has been achieved between the indigenous cultures of the Tibetan and Naxi peoples and among the Dongba religion of the Naxis, Buddhism of the Tibetans, and Christianity which was introduced in the 19th century.

Traditional manual labor, instead of modern machinery, continues to be used in salt production steps ranging from brine fetching and sunning to salt collecting and cleaning. Each brine flat is built by spreading a layer of fine soil on solid wood boards supported by thick tree trunks. This simple but practical method allows the brine to both evaporate and seep through the soil. Every morning, women fetch brine from the wells and carry buckets of brine uphill to the worksite where they initially decant the brine into a cistern. Then, purer brine is poured into the flats for evaporation until salt crystals are formed. The local people believe that this ancient method is the only way to maintain the natural energies in the salt—energies from the sun, the sea, and the mountains. This is a one-of-a-kind, time-honored salt producing method, and salt production is a major sideline occupation of the local villagers.

Salt produced at Yanjing is unique in many ways. The western bank of the Lancang River is a low gradient where the brine flats are larger in size. The reddish salt, mostly produced between March and May, is also called "peach flower salt" or "red salt." The eastern bank of the Lancang River is a thin strip of land where the brine flats are disconnected. The pure white salt produced here is called "white salt." The colors of the salts come from the earth used in the brine flats. The red salt is produced in large amounts and sold at a lower price while the white salt, produced in flats erected over an incline, is a bit more expensive because of its low output.

The Yanjing brine flats, a well-preserved ancient cultural heritage site, are regarded as "works of sunshine and wind." The natural environment of Yanjing and its unique, primitive method of salt production constitute a wondrous example of human handiwork in the landscape.

Quxur County | *3,600*
Tibet | meters above sea level

8848m

8000m

7000m

6000m
snow line

5000m

4000m

3000m

2000m

1000m

500m
200m
0m

Quxur County | *3,600*
Tibet | meters above sea level

Under the jurisdiction of Lhasa, Quxur County is 50 kilometers away from the city of Lhasa. It is situated on the lower reach of the Lhasa River on the northern bank of the Yarlung Zangbo River's middle reach in Tibet's interior. It is relatively high in the west and the east and low in the middle where the Lhasa and Yarlung Zangbo Rivers converge. Quxur in Tibetan means "waterway."

THE POWER THAT ROCKS THE RIVERS: YAK-HIDE SKIFFS OF JUNPA VILLAGE

Before joining the Yarlung Zangbo River, the Lhasa River flows past the small village of Junpa. This is the only fishing village in Tibetan Autonomous Region where the villagers have been making a living fishing for generations. Junpa in Tibetan means "to catch" or "to hold."

One day, Pema comes to the riverside and retrieves a piece of yak hide out of the river. This is the traditional way of yak hide tanning.

Pema brings together a few workmates who fish out a few pieces of yak hide and prepare to sew them together. Without drawing any lines, they give free rein to their experienced hands while cutting the yak hide. After a large piece of yak hide is cut into desired shape, they also cut the leather scraps into thin shreds to be used as cords. A whole piece of yak hide is thus sewed onto the frame of a skiff. It will be tightly attached to the frame when it is completely dry. Not a single nail is used in the shipbuilding process. A skiff comes into shape by virtue of the yak hide's tension and the joints between wood sticks. Then the workers apply local rapeseed oil to the leather boat which is ready to set sail when the yak hides are fully soaked with the oil.

With a history of more than a thousand years, this boat is called a yak-hide skiff or coracle. It is a major water-faring vessel used in some parts of China and is used by the Junpa villagers as a fishing boat. Fishing is such an important means of subsistence that a celebration is held whenever a new boat is made. Villagers carry the boats on their shoulders and join in a joyful dance accompanied by rhythmical singing. A boat sounds like a drum invested with power from the rivers.

For religious reasons, catching and eating fish is a taboo for most people living in Tibetan areas. Special traditions, however, have given rise to this only fishing village in Tibet. The locals say that fishing stories are found in their ancient folklore.

People had to make a living fishing because of the scarcity of arable land, and this way of life has continued into today.

The new boat sets sail and a new fishing trip begins. The locals begin to fish when the peach flowers are in blossom because they believe that this is the season when the fish are not only delectable but also nutritious. Boat on shoulder, a crew of two or three men set out to the river, elated by the familiar peach flower. They allow the boat to float on the water and wait for the fish to come into the net. Their catch is mostly sold to retailers at the fish market in Lhasa.

The Fishing Village of Junpa

The small fishing village of Junpa is part of Chabalang Village of the Quxur Town, the seat of Quxur County. As the only fishing village in Tibet, it is located on the southern bank of the Yarlung Zangbo River that is joined by the Lhasa River. Junpa in the Tibetan language means "catcher" or "fisherman." This is a beautiful village with a unique fishing culture. The yak-hide skiff dance is performed to celebrate the Fishing Festival in March of the Tibetan calendar.

Here the clean headwaters of the Yangtze River, the Yellow River, and the Yarlung Zangbo River teem with fish of various species. Fish dishes, however, are absent from most Tibetans' tables for religious and traditional reasons. For Tibetan Buddhists, fishing is a serious taboo. For Bon believers, fish, frogs, and other aquatic animals are associated with God Klu. No one dares to kill these animals because even physical contact with any of them is under taboo. That's why few Tibetan farmers and herdsmen eat aquatic products and still fewer work as fishermen. Among all the villages in Tibet and even the entire Qinghai-Tibet Plateau, Junpa is an exception where all the villagers make a living fishing.

Legend has it that, in ancient times, an enormous school of winged fish from the Lhasa River flew into the sky, and many earthly creatures died because the fish blocked the sun and the moon. Enraged, Buddha Sakyamuni ordered a Junpa fisherman who guarded the local lake to annihilate the flying fish and henceforth allowed him and his villagers to eat fish. The fisherman fought nine days and nights against the fish and finally won the battle. This is how the fish-eating tradition started in Junpa and the fisherman is respected by the villagers as their ancestor.

Interesting as the story is, Junpa villagers live by fishing for other reasons. Junpa is surrounded by mountains on three sides and the limited arable land can hardly support its inhabitants, so they resort to fishing for subsistence. The small village of Junpa is endowed with a horde of fish species thanks to its location at the juncture of the Lhasa River and the Yarlung Zangbo River, hence its reputation as Tibet's "fishing village."

The Lhasa River boasts a variety of fish species including "whitefish," "colored fish," "sharp-lipped fish," "bearded fish," "thin-skinned fish," "club fish," and the well-known Tibetan catfish which is almost boneless except for its backbone. As a specialty of the Lhasa River, catfish is sold at high prices in Lhasa. People fish all year round except during the Tibetan New Year and the Saga Dawa Festival. March and April are the best fishing season and July and August are the best season to catch catfish.

Junpa villagers use yak-hide skiffs for fishing. The yak-hide skiff is a light boat made by attaching four yak hides to a framed keel. Once dried, the yak hides are tightly attached to the frame, and the boat must be dried again after each use. A yak-hide skiff can carry a crew of three because its flat bottom keeps it steady on the river. The fishing net can be used by one man alone or by two men working together to catch fish.

Tibet is home to numerous rivers with low beds and dramatic seasonal changes in water level. There are also rapids running through great valleys between towering mountains, and wood boats are hardly suited for use under such conditions. Yak-hide skiffs, however, are resistant to damage by rocks because of the yak hide becomes soft and pliable when soaked. They can negotiate both shallow and deep waterways because of their lightness. Another advantage of the yak-hide skiff lies in its portability. While most non-motorized boats sailing upstream need to be pulled by boat pullers, a yak-hide skiff can even be carried by one man over rough terrain. Carrying yak-hide skiffs has not only shaped the fishermen's strong physiques but also inspired a unique highland art—the yak-hide skiff dance, which is said to be a variant of the traditional Tibetan "Yak Dance." The rhythmical and primitive yak-hide skiff dance is performed by singing and dancing men called ara, along with a group of fishermen who knock on the skiffs they carry on their shoulders. In 2008, the yak-hide skiff dance of Junpa was listed as one of China's national non-material cultural legacies.

Nyêmo County | *3,800*
Tibet | meters above sea level

The highlanders believe that each river is inhabited by gods and fishes. In a river named Tunchu in Nyêmo, however, there isn't a single fish.

An ancient watermill still operates in Tunchu River. Legend has it that the local authorities ordered the building of watermills and forbade all fish to go into Tunchu River lest they get injured. This is why the river has been fishless. But what is the purpose of these mills that have been built with so much effort?

A DIFFERENT ART: TIBETAN INCENSE MANUFACTURING

Once in a while, Tsering Dorji and his wife saw off a section of the cypress tree trunk they have saved for a long time. He cuts a mortise in the sawed-off trunk and fixes it to the watermill, which rubs the trunk against a hard surface to produce pulp. He molds the pulp into bricks and builds a stack of them to be sun-dried. Then Tsering Dorji begins to prepare a variety of medicinal substances including negi red, saffron, and musk. These are rare medicines that are required despite their high expense.

He uses a stone roller to grind the herbs into a powder and mixes it with cypress dust in water. The mushy mixture is pressed through a small hole at one end of a yak horn to form a thin line. This seems to be a simple procedure, but it takes years of practice to produce a fine line at one go. Tsering Dorji cuts the ends of these thin strips and puts them evenly on a mesh to dry. Made from precious medical substances, these Tibetan incense sticks bear the scent of highland sunshine and flowing water. Tibetan incense sticks are mostly burned as offerings to Buddha and to ward off illnesses, pests, and evil spirits.

Tsering Dorji says that some Tibetan incense smells bitter and some sweet. Good wine is neither bitter nor sweet and the same is true of good incense. Good smell purifies one's heart.

Mindroling Monastery 3,760
Tibet | meters above sea level

8848m
8000m

7000m

6000m
snow line

5000m

4000m

3000m

2000m

1000m
500m
200m
0m

Mindroling Monastery | 3,760
Tibet | meters above sea level

Built in the final years of the 10th century, Mindroling Monastery is located in Chanang County, Lhoka Prefecture, Tibet. It is one of the six great Nyingmapa Buddhist monasteries and is famous for its Tibetan incense.

Tamcho Tenzin is the abbot and transmitter of incense-making at Mindroling Monastery. The recipe of the incense made here remains a secret, and the incense is used for special purposes.

Mindroling Monastery has an ancient Buddhist academy that attracts large numbers of young monks who test their intelligence through heated debates. The class schedule is full, but there is one course which they study lightheartedly.

For these diligent young monks, the incense making course is more like an extracurricular activity. They carefully choose and weigh the spices, grind them into powders and mix them with water, and then press the mixture into fine strips.

Incense made in different places represents local manufacturing knowhow. Incense sticks made by the young monks must be checked by a senior monk before entering the final stage where they are empowered through sutra chanting. These blessed incense sticks are certainly different from other incenses made in other lands.

Tibetan Incense

Tibetan incense is one of the important vehicles for carrying down the Tibetan Buddhist tradition. An intriguingly mixed scent of herbs and ghee permeates Tibetan monasteries and homes. This smell of Tibetan incense is part of Tibet's ubiquitous religious atmosphere.

It is difficult to determine when Tibetan incense came into being. A relatively reliable story tells of Thon-mi Sambhota who introduced incense making technologies from India around the 7th century. Incense manufacturing with Tibetan characteristics thus came into being in Nyêmo near Lhasa 1,300 years ago. Thanks to the development of Buddhism and the propagation by numerous Buddhist masters, Tibetan incense has become an offering and a daily necessity for the clergy and the laity.

Tibetan incense recipes include many traditional materials with the major ingredient coming from cypress and elm tree trunks. Proportionate quantities of dozens of spices, including saffron, musk, and white, red, and purple sandalwood dusts, are mixed and kneaded. While some of the spices are produced locally, the other raw materials come from Han areas and foreign countries. Cypress trees, the major ingredient of Tibetan incense, cannot grow at high altitudes, so they need to be transported into Tibet over long distances. Some of the spices come from central China, India, or southeastern countries, so Tibetan incense can be regarded as a product of multiple cultures.

Tibetan incense is an indispensible part of the Tibetan people's daily life. A Tibetan incense recipe includes at least two to three ingredients up to a few dozen spices. In the history of traditional Tibetan incense making, Toinba Village of Nyêmo, Doilung Dêqên in Lhasa's western outskirts, and Mindroling Monastery of Lhoka have become the three major locations of Tibetan incense manufacturing.

The first step of Tibetan incense making is to cut a cypress tree trunk into smaller sections and remove the bark. A wood shaft is driven into a hole cut in the middle of a trunk so this chunk of wood can be attached to the watermill. The wood is scraped against rough stone slabs day and night until it becomes a pulp. Next, the pulp is made into bricks and sun-dried. Drying time and moisture of the bricks are vital: dried wood powder will be blown away by wind if the pulp is not wet enough, and a longer drying time is needed if the pulp is too wet; the pulp will lose much of its aroma if it is sun-dried for too long. Therefore, rich experience is needed in this second step. Step three is to crush the bricks into a powder, mix it with spices and then knead them into a dough-like mixture. Dozens of spices of varying colors, smells, and effects are used in this step. Step four is to press the mixture through a small hole at one end of a yak horn to form a fine strip of incense. This step is a test of the incense maker's skills and patience. Step five, the last step, is to sun-dry the incense sticks. This must be done in a place with a low temperature and enough sunshine. The incense cannot be exposed in hot sun for long periods of time. In two or three days, the incense sticks are packed as finished products.

The Qing Dynasty saw frequent communications between Tibet and central China, and Tibetan incense used to be a major tribute item. When introduced into China's interior, Tibetan incense soon became popular among the upper class. Today, Tibetan incense is increasingly known to the world thanks to tourism development, and Tibetan incense sticks have become a popular tourist souvenir.

Taking Up and Putting Down: Mandala of Saga Dawa

Bucket in hand, lama Tenzin from the Mindroling Monastery is walking against the sandy wind. He is travelling across a desert to fetch a type of special sand.

A kind of soft rock is found on a mountain near the Yarlung Zangbo River. These rocks are crushed and sifted to produce fine grains of snow-white sand. Lama Tenzin scoops the sand into his bucket and goes back to his monastery.

The white sand is dyed yellow, green, red, blue, and black, each color having a special implication. The young monks burn incense and chant the sutras to commence an important part of their curriculum under instruction by their masters.

The floor of the main hall is thoroughly cleaned before chalk lines are drawn on the floor to form a meticulously drafted pattern for visualization, called yantra. The monks have already learned the pattern by heart; the work is done by their experienced hands. Colored sands fall from between their fingers and the mental image becomes a picture. More than 40 monks, working from the four corners, concentrate on constructing a mystical pattern.

The construction of such a pattern with the fine sands is called dkyil khor in Tibetan Buddhism, and the finished structure is better known as sand mandala. The mandala is regarded by Tibetan Buddhists as the abode, the city, and the cosmos of Buddha. It is said that Buddha Sakyamuni also worked with his disciples to create mandalas. The finished sand mandala is a magnificent, sublime pattern. One can hardly believe that such a colorful cosmos is made of sands if one hasn't seen it with his own eyes.

The finished sand mandala is ready to be worshipped by Buddhists at the Saga Dawa festival which is celebrated in April of the Tibetan calendar. This is the month that commemorates Buddha Sakyamuni's birth, awakening, and nirvana. Tibetan Buddhists believe that chanting sutras, doing good deeds, and freeing captured animals in this month can bring them many times more merits and virtues than they can otherwise get in other times.

More people have been buying fish at the Lhasa fish market lately. A family from Lhasa buys 3,000 yuan's worth of fish which they put in oxygenated bags. They drive along the Yarlung Zangbo River until they arrive at an open section of the river, where they stop the car and open the bags. Chanting sutras quietly, they free the fish back into water. They believe that they will reap good fruits for their good karma of freeing fish on this day.

Sonorous trumpets and drums announce the final arrival of the Saga Dawa festival. Incense sticks in hand, people gather around the mandala and wait quietly to witness the change and disappearance of a colorful sand cosmos. When the ritual is finished, the holy palace which the monks have so painstakingly built is quickly destroyed by the hands that created it. The colorful sands will be collected, bottled, and then spread into rivers to pray for good luck in the coming year.

What is taken up with effort can also be put down without reluctance; what is built and rebuilt can also be destroyed once and again; whatever part they have played in a grand, luxuriant enterprise, the sand grains will ultimately return to being what they are. These are probably what the sand mandala symbolizes.

Sand Mandala

The Sand mandala is a unique Tibetan Buddhist art. The mandala is a spiritual symbol used in Buddhism to represent the universe. It originated from ancient esoteric meditation practices in India. In order to ward off evil spirits, the monks would build a round or square mound in their dharma practice venue and invite Buddhas of the past, present, and future to witness their efforts. The mounds topped with painted Buddha images were the early forms of sand mandalas.

The Tibetan phrase for sand mandala is dkyil khor, literally meaning "mandala of colored sands." This exquisite art has been handed down from generation to generation since Buddha Sakyamuni himself taught his disciples how to construct sand mandalas. It has been preserved in Tibet since its introduction in the 11th century.

The sands used to build the mandala are made by grinding special rocks. The white sand can be dyed black, blue, red, yellow, and green. Besides their black and white colors, sands of the remaining four colors appear in dark, regular, and light shades so that there are altogether 14 types of colored sands available for use. Generally speaking, the five basic colors of blue, yellow, red, green, and white correspond to the "Five Buddhas" and five wisdoms.

The building of a sand mandala involves cooperative work of several skilled lamas. They draw chalk circles and perpendicular and diagonal lines which form the basic pattern on the floor. They draw geometric measurements within the basic pattern and start working gradually from the center toward the edges. Each step must be completed by strictly following instructions specified in the Tantra texts. Lamas building the mandala must receive strict training; they must bear in mind each detail of the procedure and refrain from improvisation.

Constructing the sand mandala is a meticulous process requiring considerable effort. The builders can spread fine sand grains on the floor or use a funnel to apply the sands onto the pattern. Whatever method is used, concentration is needed to carefully lay down the sands. Each design must be finished at one stretch because any careless move may ruin what is already achieved. Depending on size, mandalas take days or even months to construct. A completed sand mandala is a colorful artwork in which blocs of colored sand are deployed to give perfect expression to religious implications.

Sand mandalas are constructed in varying sizes. A large mandala covers about one square meter and larger ones can be five to six square meters in size. A sand mandala looks like a luxurious tapestry or an exquisite architectural model. Lamas use large amounts of sand to build colorful Buddha worlds for grand religious rituals. After the rituals, however, these beautiful sand paintings created with great effort will be destroyed without a moment of hesitation. They will be whisked away in a matter of a few minutes and the sands will be collected and bottled. Half of the sands will be given to Buddhists participating in the ritual and the rest will be dumped into nearby rivers and streams so that the blessings can be carried into the oceans and then to each corner of the world.

Sand is the basic element that constitutes the terrestrial realm. The sand mandala is both beautiful and fragile, and its transient existence perfectly represents the ephemerality of the world. This may be exactly why sand mandalas are a thought-provoking art.

Chomo | 3,500
Tibet | meters above sea level

8848m
8000m

7000m

6000m
snow line

5000m

4000m

3000m

2000m

1000m

500m
200m
0m

Chomo | 3,500
Tibet | meters above sea level

Under the jurisdiction of Shigatse in south Tibet, Chomo County is 390 kilometers away from Shigatse and 580 kilometers away from Lhasa. Chomo in Tibetan means "eddy river valley" or "valley of rapid currents." As the reputed "riverine southland of Tibet," Chomo County features beautiful landscapes, congenial climate, plentiful precipitation, and abundant natural resources. Situated 4,360 meters above sea level, Chomo is the "highest county" in the world. It boasts rich natural and cultural tourism resources and prosperous border trade.

HEALING POWERS OF THE MIRACULOUS EAGLE HOT SPRINGS

This small town in Chomo County looks more like a hospital. Sixteen-year-old Pema is suffering from osteonecrosis of the femur; she doesn't want to get married with a lame leg. She has heard of the miraculous treatment provided by a hospital in this small town, so she has arrived here with her mother.

The doctor gives her an X-ray check and asks her to eat nutritious foods. The doctor warns that her chance of recovery is slim if she doesn't take her diet seriously. Pema's physician in charge is named Basang whose prescriptions invariably include bathing in the hot spring.

According to legend, a broken-winged eagle fell into the hot spring and miraculously recovered from the injury after staying in the spring for seven days. This is how this hot spring has come to be called "Eagle Spring."

People come to Eagle Spring by using a convenient transportation network. The

hot spring bathers say that the water here is clean enough to be drinkable. With its name spread from mouth to mouth, the small town is crowded with people seeking treatment.

Twelve different hot springs are scattered through the area, and some of them won't release water unless knocked with stones. It is said that each spring can help treat certain illnesses. People go from one spring to another, chatting and enjoying the hot bath and thus turning the springs into social networks. The young girl Pema has met many people here and gained knowledge of society. People come and go every day, and new comers arrive with crutches and baggage. Many crutches dumped at the perimeter bear witness to the miraculous effects of Eagle Spring. Having bathed in the hot springs, many people find themselves recovering from leg diseases. A patient tells Basang that his leg still hurts. Basang assures him that things won't go worse; he only needs to walk slowly.

Dr. Basang has always wanted to know why the hot springs have such miraculous healing effects. Attempting to look at the mysterious spring water from a scientific point of view, he collects a water sample and plans to have it tested in a lab. The results show that the water indeed contains some minerals beneficial to human health.

Basang often climbs the hills to look for medicinal herbs in the "medicine valley." Basang thinks to himself that these herbs and substances may account for the curative effects of the hot springs.

Seeing the patients enjoying leisurely games and sunbathing, Dr. Basang realizes that the best therapy may have come from the environment. Here people don't regard themselves as patients. They bathe in the hot springs and bask in the sun; they chat and take medicines; they play games or just relax and sit there in a trance. They live and recover in a natural environment. On top of the mountain, people's good wishes are spread by the fluttering prayer flags and tsampa tossed high above. All these taken together constitute a beneficial influence which helps patients to recover.

There are over 600 hot springs on the Qinghai-Tibet Plateau, but not all of them are suitable for bathing.

Batang 3,300
Sichuan meters above sea level

8848m

8000m

7000m

6000m
snow line

5000m

4000m

3000m

2000m

1000m

500m
200m
0m

Batang | *3,300*
Sichuan | meters above sea level

Batang County is located in the western part of Garzê Prefecture, Sichuan. The Tsopaggou National Forest Park of Batang boasts unique natural conditions, complex terrain, and diverse landscapes; it is the "pearl of China's greater Shangrila eco-tourism zone"—a gallery of natural beauties.

A HIGHLAND LOVE STORY

Batang has a geothermal zone with hot springs distributed everywhere. Water erupting from geysers can reach 90 degrees Celsius. The mountain air here is warmed by high-temperature water erupting from the springs.

Lhamo, a college student spending her summer vacation in her hometown, comes along with a bamboo basket. She seems to have something on her mind lately.

There are several eggs in her basket. She lays the basket in an opening of the hot spring. Eggs cooked in the hot spring are soft on the inside and flavorful on the outside. Today, she cooks these eggs for her loved one.

On the green pasture at the foot of the mountain, a herd of yaks are grazing on grass. "Dad, I am going to herd the yaks," says Shirap to his father before leaving home. His father has asked him to herd the yaks to lush pastures.

Shirap works in the city. Today he is going to meet his girlfriend under the pretext of herding. He is taking care of the yaks when Lhamo arrives with a basket. She waves her hand and says hello.

Shirap runs toward Lhamo. "Let's sit here," he says. The young people sit on the grass to have a chat. "When did you come back?" Shirap asks Lhamo.

"A few days ago," Lhamo answers.

"Where shall we go?" asks Shirap.

"Let's walk around the lake," says Lhamo. "I've brought some eggs."

"Eggs? Where did you cook them?"

"Over there," says Lhamo pointing into the distance.

"Let me try one," says Shirap.

"Is it cooked?" asks Lhamo.

"Yes. It tastes good."

Shirap hums a tune delightedly. The two of them walk slowly around the sacred lake. They pray in their hearts; their love is growing.

Their hometown Batang is a beautiful place with the sacred mountain and forests in the distance and the crystal-clear Tsopag Lake nearby. By hollering at the lake's edge one can summon a school of fish. Shirap hollers and fish shoals swim toward him as expected.

"Here they come!" shouts Lhamo excitedly. "Here come so many fish!"

Lhamo and Shirap toss bits of food into the lake and more fish gather around in the transparent water. If she graduates as planned, says Lhamo, she will return home because she wants to do something for the folks.

Shirap is delighted to hear that. The good-natured young man is not disposed to express himself, so he tosses wind-horse paper into the sky. The colored prayer sheets carry his wishes and dreams toward the sacred mountain and lake.

Wonderful feelings buried in the heart grow like the lush forest. The beautiful scenes of their hometown obviate the need to exchange loving words. Tacit communication takes place through the medium of the natural environment.

Geothermal Springs in Tibet

Boasting the largest number of hot springs in China, Tibet is dotted with numerous large and small thermal springs that represent a nearly full range of the world's geothermal water types, such as hydrothermal explosion craters, intermittent springs, hot rivers, highland boiling springs, hot river fountains, boiling mud pools, and geothermal steam areas. Tibet owes these geothermal springs to its special geology and geography: they are the gift of nature.

Hot spring baths are an important type of therapy in Tibetan medicine. According to the late-8th-century medical classic *Four Tantras* authored by Yuthok Yontan Gonpo, founder of Tibetan medicine, hot springs are therapeutically effective in strengthening vitality, prolonging life, dispelling coldness, and restoring beauty. Hot spring water as a medical substance can be used both internally and externally. Tibetan medical theories hold that recurrence of illnesses takes place when peach flowers are in blossom and hot spring baths can reveal the symptoms of an illness before it develops. Hot spring baths in fall, on the other hand, can help cure the illnesses.

The time-honored hot spring culture of Tibet has become integrated with medicine and religion. Therapeutic hot spring bathing is very popular among the Tibetans because it is convenient and effective and has no toxic side-effects. Ancient Tibetans found minerals like sulfur, calcite, anthracites, fibroferrite, and brag-zhun around hot springs and believed that it was these heat-producing substances that warmed and formed the hot springs. The odor, color, and medical effects of the hot spring water come from its mineral contents. Different types of water are used to treat different illnesses: yellowish and bitter sulfur water is used to treat rash and leprosy; clean and odorless calcite water expels latent heat and is used to treat stomach ulcer and kidney problems; darkish and turbid fibroferrite water is used to treat tumors and chronic gastritis; purple and bitter brag-zhun water is used to treat stomach ulcer, gout, uremia, and dropsy; and tarry smelling anthracitic water is used to treat indigestion. Generally speaking, regular hot spring baths serve as an efficacious treatment for dermatitis, limb stiffness, and spine curvature.

Shigatse has more hot springs than other parts of Tibet. The best-known hot spring clusters in Tibet are the Yangpachen, Lhazê, Bibilong, and Jiaga Hot Springs—three of which are found in Shigatse. These hot springs are valuable resources for tourism and medicine in Tibet. Large numbers of hot springs are also found in Tibet's neighboring regions like the Batang Hot Springs in Sichuan.

The Third Pole

ཨཱ།འཛམ་གླིང་ཡང་རྩེ།

I CAN'T JUST LIVE FOR MYSELF;
I NEED TO THINK ABOUT THEIR
FUTURE BECAUSE THESE APPLE
TREES ARE ALSO THEIR PROPERTY.

CHILDREN OF GREAT MOUNTAINS

The Qinghai-Tibet Plateau has been created by collisions of continental plates, which have raised great mountain ranges in the earth's crust. This region of successive crustal upheavals is known as the Roof of the World. Snowy mountains and alpine meadows exist alongside forests and valleys, giving rise to a wide range of human activities. People regard the mountains as sacred abodes of gods and their own home.

Rongbuk Monastery | 5,154
Tibet | meters above sea level

8848m
8000m
7000m
6000m
snow line
5000m
4000m
3000m
2000m
1000m
500m
200m
0m

Rongbuk Monastery | **5,154**
Tibet | meters above sea level

The Rongbuk Monastery is a Nyingmapa temple built in 1899. Located in Basong Town, Dingri County, Shigatse City, Tibet, it is perched at the head of Rongbuk Ravine, where eastern and western ridges join at Qomolangma's northern foot. At the altitude of 5,154 meters and only 20 kilometers away from Mt. Qomolangma, it is the highest monastery in the world and serves as the base camp for mountaineers climbing the mountain's north face. Looking southward from here, Mt. Qomolangma presents a majestic view which tourists adore and photographers like to capture. The mani cairn in front of the monastery often foregrounds photos of Mt. Qomolangma taken here. In front of the

PRAYING FOR MT. QOMOLANGMA MOUNTAINEERS: NGAWANG SANGGYE AND THE RONGBUK MONASTERY

main hall stands an opera stage with carved beams and painted rafters where the lamas put on pageants for local audiences on important holidays.

Ngawang Sanggye has been living in the Rongbuk Monastery for more than 20 years. He has been taking care of this sacred grotto which is part of the monastery. While sitting quietly in this grotto he can feel the presence of great Buddhist masters. Here he diligently learns and practices Buddhist dharma.

Five auspicious goddesses are said to be living in the Himalayas behind the monastery. "Qomolangma," the highest mountain of the Himalayas, means the "Third Goddess" in Tibetan. Rising 8844 meters above sea level, it is surrounded by more than 40 mountains above the altitude of 7,000 meters. This is the highest point on earth, the hometown of snow and ice.

Mt. Qomolangma was recognized as the highest mountain on earth in 1852.

Mountaineers have been climbing it ever since, and more than 4,000 of them have reached its peak.

For Ngawang Sanggye, Mt. Qomolangma is the abode of gods. He was married with children before he began to live a monastic life. His three sons work with mountaineer clubs and his second son has reached the peak of Mt. Qomolangma seven times.

His youngest son Tashi, a cook working at a mountaineering club, pays regular visits to his hermitic dharma-practicing father. Today, as Tashi is about to make another visit, his mother prepares supplies for his father and wants him to assure his father that family support is always available whenever anything is needed.

Walking along the stone steps, Tashi comes to his father's room. He hands his father the medicines he has brought and says: "Take these pills after meals and stick these patches on your knees." His father tells him that sometimes his knees hurt badly. Tashi opens the wrapping and applies a medicinal patch to his father's right knee. "Please take care of yourself," says Tashi to his father. "Call home if you need anything."

Father and son sit on the hilltop. "I want to climb the Qomalangma," Tashi reveals his yearning. "I think I can see everything at the peak, right?"

"Yes, you can see most of the world there," says his father. "But things will appear very small to you."

"I've been working for the mountaineers for two years," continues Tashi. "Now my biggest wish is to climb the Qomalangma like my brother. That must be very exciting."

"Do it with care," says his father. "It takes great efforts to get to the top. Be extremely careful when you climb it. That's my wish."

Tashi is gone, and Lama Ngawang Sanggye continues his lone caretaking duties at the monastery, praying for each mountaineer braving the height of Mt. Qomolangma. "It is the brave who climb the Qomolangma," he says. "My strongest wish is that they will be safe and successful." Lama Ngawang Sanggye is the single individual who lives closest to Mt. Qomolangma.

The Himalayas and Mt. Qomolangma

The Himalayas are the highest mountains in the world, comprising a large number of approximately parallel massifs stretching from east to west. This range, stretching 2,400 kilometers long and 200-300 kilometers wide, is mostly situated on the border areas of China, India, and Nepal. Most of the mountain peaks are over 6,200 meters above sea level. Qomolangma, the highest mountain in the world, rises 8,844 meters above sea level on the China-Nepal border. Situated in the middle part of the Himalayas, it is surrounded by 42 mountains, each of which is 7,000 meters above sea level and four of which rise more than 8,000 meters above sea level. The Sanskrit word Himalaya means "the abode of snow."

The Himalayas can be divided into three belts from the south to the north. The southern belt at altitudes between 700 and 1,000 meters features hilly terrain of the range's foothills. The middle belt at altitudes between 3,500 and 4,000 meters is known as the "Lesser Himalaya." The northern belt consists of many great mountains which form the Himalayas' major mountain chain with a width of 50 to 60 kilometers. These mountains have an average altitude of 6,000 meters, dozens of which rise 7,000 meters above sea level including Mt. Qomolangma. All these mountains are snow-covered all year round.

As the commanding peak of the Himalayas, Mt. Qomolangma is situated on the China-Nepal border area with its north face in Tibet and its south face in Nepal. It is a mighty, majestic mountain which defines a unique geographical region. The temperature at its top remains below minus 30 degrees Celsius. Some parts of it are covered with permanent snow; glaciers, ice slopes, and ice spire forests are seen everywhere.

Mt. Qomolangma in its full glory is so impressive that it appears on the ten-yuan note of the fourth series of the Renminbi issued by the People's Republic of China.

Mêdog *1,200*
Tibet   meters above sea level

8848m

8000m

7000m

6000m
snow line

5000m

4000m

3000m

2000m

1000m

500m
200m
0m

Mêdog | *1,200*
Tibet | meters above sea level

Under the jurisdiction of Nyingchi city, Mêdog County is located in southeastern Tibet with Mêdog Town being its seat. Specifically, Mêdog is situated at the southern foot of the Himalayas' east end, on the lower reach of the Yarlung Zangbo River. Most of the local residents are from the Menba and Lhoba ethnic groups. The great mountains of Namjagbarwa and Gyala Peri are situated in Mêdog. As the highest mountains of the Eastern Himalayas, their snow-capped peaks contrast with the subtropical vegetation on the southern slope of the Himalayas. The major section of the famous Yarlung Zangbo River is also found in Mêdog. Situated at the lowest point in Tibet, Mêdog is endowed

ANCIENT TASTES: STONE POTS OF MÊDOG

with optimal natural conditions: compared with other areas of Tibet, Mêdog has the most congenial climate, the most plentiful rainfall, and the best preserved eco-system. Entering Mêdog, one is exposed to a series of splendid views where the transition from cold alpine landscapes to tropical rain forests can be witnessed during a few short hours of travel.

The Yarlung Zangbo Canyon, the longest and deepest canyon in the world, is the most important passageway for humid airflow to enter the Qinghai-Tibet Plateau. Here can be found lush vegetation and plentiful rainfall. Mêdog, "the hidden lotus," is located deep in the valley.

Early one morning, the Menba man Dönhong hurries downhill while the good weather holds. Recently he has started bringing his youngest son with him wherever he goes.

This section of the canyon is situated right in a rainy belt. Many people come to the cliffs of the canyon to quarry a certain stone in good weather. This kind of rock, known as soapstone, is used by the locals to make cooking pots because of its soft texture. The

making of stone cooking pots is an ancient craft handed down through the generations. Dönhong wants his youngest son to carry down the family tradition of stone pot making.

Dönhong and his son use picks to quarry chunks of rock which will be used to make stone pots. In order to lighten the load they need carry home, they start the first step of the pot-making procedure. Hewn by axe and roughed out by pick, large rocks are reduced to pot-size stones. Then they carry the stones home in bamboo baskets in order to process them further at home.

The father and son negotiate the mountain trails agilely despite the heavy loads on their backs. This is not a hard job for them as they are quite used to walking on steep slopes while carrying heavy stones.

Back home, they are going to work further on the stones. Stone pot making requires skillful expertise to apply just the right degree of strength to each scraping and hewing movement. Patience and manual dexterity are needed to carve thin, even, and smooth surfaces. It is said that soft soapstone pots will harden once they are taken away from Mêdog.

As his son carves a stone pot, Dönhong gives him guidance: "Smooth the rough surface on the inside and try to make it even and smooth."

Mêdog was the last Chinese county to be accessed by road. Stone pot making has almost become a cottage industry since the removal of difficulties in transportation. A stone pot is sold at one to two thousand Chinese yuan, so Dönhong believes that stone pot making is a promising trade. He feels more confident in persuading his son to learn this art.

"Now, hold and feel it," says Dönhong to his son. "Turn it around to see if its surface feels smooth. Check its fullness, and see if the handle is shaped well. Knock it to hear how it sounds. If the sounds are bright and clear, it is a good pot."

Soapstone pots are an indispensable part of a Menba person's life from the time he or she is born. Soups cooked with soapstone pots taste delectably mellow and are said to be amazingly beneficial to the human heart and bones.

Dönhong's father was one of the most famous soapstone pot makers in Mêdog. The stone pot used by Dönhong's family has been handed down from past generations.

Dönhong's wife has brewed some yellow wine using a soapstone pot. This wine is brewed from a mixture of corn and chicken feet millet. It not only treats rheumatism caused by spells of rainy weather but also brings hours of conviviality.

Dönhong says to his son: "[Soapstone pot making] is our major source of income. It will be worth your while to learn the pot making craft our ancestors handed down to us. Put your heart into it and don't be afraid of hardships."

"Does that mean to do it with devotion?"

"As long as you are determined to do it, you will know what to do next," says Dönhong encouragingly. "Always take it seriously. Mastering a craft is necessary to make a living. You've done quite a good job today."

Dönhong's soapstone pots have been gaining popularity recently and orders are coming from restaurants on the other side of the mountain. It remains challenging, however, to transport their pots outside the village which is located halfway up the mountain. Their stone pots need to be carried by horse caravans that trudge along winding paths to the county seat, after which they are transported outside Mêdog on highways.

"This unique craft has a long history in our town," says Dönhong. "I've been making a living making stone pots. There's nothing special about it, but I believe what I have done is the best for me."

Lulang | 3,700
Tibet | meters above sea level

8848m
8000m

7000m

6000m
snow line

5000m

4000m

3000m

2000m

1000m

500m
200m
0m

Lulang | *3,700*
Tibet | meters above sea level

At the altitude of 3,700 meters, Lulang is located in deep mountains on the Sichuan-Tibet Highway about 80 kilometers away from Bayi Town, Nyingchi City. The shrubs and thick spruce and pine forests on the mountains on both sides of the highway form the "Lulang Sea of Trees." Gurgling creeks and streams wind through evenly contoured meadows between the mountains. Tens of thousands of wild flowers are in full blossom in the flowering season. Renowned as a "natural oxygen bar" and "wild life gene pool," Lulang in Tibetan means "the valley of the Dragon King" and "the abode of gods."

Mêdog soapstone pots are brought here and used in the alpine forests of Lulang, outside of the rainy belt. A few Tibetan women are searching through the meadow plants, and once in a while they dig up the roots of a flowering herb. It turns out that they are looking for 'palm ginseng,' the tubers of fragrant orchids (Gymnadenia conopsea), a rare and precious herbal medicine only found on the highland. These tubers are washed and cooked in a stone pot with a dozen other plants and slices of local Tibetan chicken. After three hours of cooking, a chicken stew is ready to be served. Mêdog soapstone pots and an array of forest specialties combine to produce ancient yet fresh flavors to satisfy people's taste buds.

The Yarlung Zangbo Grand Canyon

Flowing from west to east to where Mainling County borders Mêdog County, the Yarlung Zangbo River is stopped by Namjagbarwa that rises 7,782 meters above sea level, making it the highest mountain in the Eastern Himalayas. The Yarlung Zangbo River is forced to change course here to form a spectacular U bend. Chinese scientists conducted a research project here in 1994. According to data provided by China's State Bureau of Surveying and Mapping, the "Yarlung Zangbo Grand Canyon" starts in the north at the Datogka Village of Mainling County and ends in the south at Batsoka Village of Mêdog County. The canyon is 504.6 kilometers long and attains an average depth of 2,268 meters, with its lowest point being 6,009 meters beneath the rim. Longer than the Grand Canyon of the Colorado River and deeper than the Colca Canyon of Peru, it is regarded as the number one canyon in the world. In September 1988, the State Council of China approved its official name as the "Yarlung Zangbo Grand Canyon."

Mêdog Soapstone Pots

Mêdog soapstone pots are produced in Mêdog County, which is Tibet's southeasternmost county as well as the last Chinese county on the Yarlung Zangbo River before it flows into India. As the last Chinese county to have road access, Mêdog was connected with the outside world by a highway completed in October 2013.

Harsh geography and frequent natural disasters of the Yarlung Zangbo Grand Canyon have set Mêdog apart from the outside world, making it an isolated arcadia. People from outside regard it as a place of mystery, and Buddhists call it "Boyu Pemako," meaning the "hidden array of lotuses."

Beshing Town of Mêdog is where the soapstone pots were originally produced. The locals quarry soapstone on the cliffs of Mt. Namjagbarwa and use primitive tools to carve the rocks into cooking pots. It is said that the soapstone is so soft that it yields to steel knives like clay but will become as hard as iron once it is taken away from Mêdog. No explanation has been formulated to account for such peculiarity of the soapstone found in Mêdog.

Soapstone used to make cooking pots is quarried on Mt. Namjagbarwa, which is the "father of ice-topped mountains." The stones are mostly quarried on the cliffs in July and August and then carried downhill by yaks and horses. They must be immersed in the Yarlung Zangbo River for one month before the craftsmen begin to work on them.

Soapstone pots are mostly light or dark grey in color. Shaped like buckets of various sizes, a large pot has a diameter of about 30 centimeters, a medium-sized 20 centimeters, and a small one 10 centimeters. The bottom of a pot can be flat or round. Soapstone pots can be used as hotpots and are ideal utensils for cooking soups, rice, meats, and vegetables because of their high-heat endurance and non-stick surface that does not discolor. Foods cooked in soapstone pots are palatable and soups are thick and tasty. The locals believe that the longer a pot is used, the better its health-promoting benefits. Foods cooked in soapstone pots have remarkable salutary effects on hypertension and cardiovascular and cerebrovascular diseases.

Mêdog soapstone pots are valuable products, useful in any kitchenware collection, because of the nutritious, delicious dishes that can be prepared in them, and because of the unique material and craftsmanship involved in their making.

Mainling | 3,700
Tibet | meters above sea level

Mainling | 3,700
Tibet | meters above sea level

Under the jurisdiction of Nyingchi, Mailing County is located between the Nyainqêntanglha Mountains and the Himalayas in southeastern Tibet. It abuts on India to the south with a borderline of 180 kilometers. High in the west and low in the east, Mainling County is situated in the valley of the Yarlung Zangbo River's middle reach. It abounds in tourism resources including the "Yarlung Zangbo Grand Canyon," Mt. Namjagbarwa that rises 7,782 meters above sea level, the Nanyi Lhoba Village, and the virgin forests of Nanyi Ravine. The Yarlung Zangbo River flows from west to east across "Mainling," which means "land of medicines" in the Tibetan language.

HANDING DOWN LHOBA FOLKLORE: GRANDPA'S CONCERNS

Centering on the Yarlung Zangbo Grand Canyon, vast forests cover the eastern part of the Qinghai-Tibet Plateau. The Lhoba people live in the southern valleys of the Himalayas. These ethnic people used to make a living by hunting wild animals but most of them have changed jobs because nature reserves have been established and hunting is banned. Their hearts, however, remain deeply rooted in the forests.

At the foot of the mountains, each family lives in a government-subsidized house, but hunter Lotun prefers living in the mountains. He is high-spirited today because his grandson Gachin is coming to spend the weekend with him. He puts on a fur cape, ties a belt around the waist, and leaves home sword in hand. He is making preparations to welcome his grandson.

Moso bamboo is the primary material used to make tools. He cuts many thin bamboos and says that in their tradition, hunters shot bears and wild boars with bamboo bows and arrows and captured other wild animals with traps made from bamboo. Lotun carries back a bunch of moso bamboo stems and cuts them into thin strips.

The Lhoba people's history is orally handed down in forms of epics and songs. Old Lotun is a propagator of this tradition. He habitually sings old hunting songs of the Lhoba people while making bamboo baskets.

Lotun makes some toys he played as a boy in case his grandson feels bored. His grandson Gachin is ten years old now and it's been quite a while since his last visit.

A crystal-clear stream flows slowly through a glen. Lotun carefully places the trap he made yesterday in a shallow part of the stream and secures it with a stone on the top.

Lotun goes into the mountains with his grandson. "Are there any bears in winter?" asks Gachin curiously.

"No, bears hibernate in winter," answers Lotun. "We see all the animals only in summer."

Everything seems so new to Gachin on his arrival. He carries fodder for the yaks, watches Grandpa milking the yak, and plays with the puppy. Very soon, things become boring to him and he begins to play his handheld game machine. Grandpa thinks it is time to show his grandson something interesting.

Grandpa leads Gachin to a tree and hands him something made from bamboo. He sets the trap and explains to Gachin how it works: "Birds will fly over to peck the apple and get caught by the bamboo clip. Try it."

Half an apple hangs from the trap. Gachin holds the clip with a stick and touches the trigger with a twig. The device catches the twig with a clap.

"Interesting?"

"Yes!"

Gachin becomes more interested. Excited, Grandpa decides to give a show of his special expertise. He takes out his bow and arrows and says to Gachin: "Let me show you how to aim at the bull's eye. This is the way to bend the bow and shoot the arrow."

In Lhoba traditions, any man who kills a large animal like the bear, wild boar, or bison will be highly respected by others.

Grandpa looks very excited. He is still very strong and vigorous although he hasn't hunted for decades. Each arrow he shoots hits the bull's eye, but Gachin doesn't seem to quite understand why Grandpa is in such high spirits.

It's about dinner time now. Old Lotun goes with his grandson into the forest to check their catch. He says that he wants to teach the younger generations everything about Lhoba culture including folk customs relating to daily life and production: cuisine, housing, travelling, and working.

Lotun and his grandson have gathered many mountain morels on the mountain and now they have arrived at the stream to check their catch. Removing the stone weight from the bamboo trap, Grandpa finds quite a few fish flapping in the trap. This is quite a good catch for them and will make a hearty hunter's meal.

Back in the cottage, Grandpa cleans the fish, skewers a few fish sprinkled with ground chilies, and grills them over the fire. Mountain morels sprinkled with salt are also skewered. The rest of the fish are placed in the pot with spices to cook a thick, fragrant soup.

"We had no lighters in the past," says Grandpa to Gachin. "We had to bring flints to make fire if we wanted to cook our meals on the mountain."

"You couldn't make a fire if there was no dry firewood around, could you?"

"No, and that's why we had to find a cave near our hunting place."

This is the moment Lotun has been waiting for, a moment when he can teach his grandson how to survive in the forest. Gachin may not understand everything, but it's been a dream of Lotun to personally tell his grandson about hunting and forest lore.

"What did you wear on your feet?" asks Gachin.

"We wore no shoes. We travelled across mountains and rivers barefoot... The fish is about cooked."

The grilled fish smells great. Lotun removes the fish skewer from the fire and hands Gachin a piece of fish. Grandpa and grandson are enjoying their dinner. "Fish in rivers and mushrooms in mountains are what our Lhoba ancestors give to our tribes," says Grandpa to Gachin. "Pheasants and other animals are generous presents the mountain gods give to us humans. Can you remember what I just said?"

"Yeah," says Gachin nodding.

This is what old Lotun tells his grandson over and again each time they meet. He believes that someday Gachin will understand what he says.

The short weekend is over and Lotun walks with Gachin on his way back. Gachin returns to his way of life, but they have made an appointment for next week.

Lhoba People

As a Chinese ethnic group, Lhoba people mostly live in Pemako in southeastern Tibet. Their population is small in comparison with other ethnic groups in China. The Tibetan word Lhoba means "Southern People." Most Lhoba people live in the alpine valleys to the west of the Yarlung Zangbo River. As of the mid-20th century, they had been identified as a primitive society in its final stage of development. They were an agrarian society with hunting being another important source of subsistence. The ancient tradition of sharing large game animals continues to this day.

Lhoba people hand down their culture by means of oral traditions. They have their own spoken language, but Tibetan is used in their writing system.

The Lhoba people's customs and life style indicate strong Tibetan influence. Their cuisine and cooking methods are largely the same as those of Tibetan farmers. Their favorite foods include grilled and dried meats, yak milk curd, and buckwheat cakes. In particular, they like pasty millet balls, and hot chili is consumed as a favorite spice. Most Lhoba people like drinking not only highland barley liquor but also corn liquor. In the past, they extracted poison from herbs and killed wild animals with poisoned arrows. They would take hunting trips in groups and share game animals equally among all the tribe members.

Different Lhoba tribes traditionally celebrate the New Year on different dates because of their wide distribution and lack of access to roads. In general, the New Year is celebrated after the fall reaping, so the celebrations are thus centered on harvest, demonstrating their readiness to see the old year out and the New Year in. Before the New Year arrives, people pound rice, brew liquor, and slaughter pigs and sheep. Better-off families may even slaughter yaks. Slaughtered domestic animals are shredded, and pieces of meat with skin are offered to other tribesmen as presents. Many Lhoba tribes have maintained the ancient tradition of "tribal gathering" where people from the same tribe, young and old, men and women, come together to feast on wine and meat dishes. They sit on the ground and eat and drink together while enjoying recreational activities.

Lhoba people have long inhabited highland valleys, and their bold and forthright characters are manifest in their costumes. A Lhoba woman typically wears a collarless linen jacket, a calfskin cape, and a tight sheath skirt. Lhoba women pay great attention to their ornaments and usually wear finger rings, silver or copper wrist bangles, dozens of necklaces, and cowries tied in clusters hanging from the waist. The weight of a woman's ornaments may amount to a few kilograms.

Lhoba men's clothing shows features of hunter's lifestyle. A Lhoba man usually wears a black-wool pullover and a bison cape. When a man goes outside he usually carries his bow and sword, which give him a powerful, imposing appearance.

Lhoba people hold their traditions in high esteem. In 2008, Mainling Lhoba costumes were added to China's second non-material heritage list and Mainling Lhoba cloth weaving was added to Tibet's first non-material heritage list. Constant efforts have been made to win places on the local non-material heritage list for Lhoba language, folktales, drinking songs, bamboo utensil making, wedding and funeral customs, and totem culture, making it possible for these to be handed down from generation to generation among Lhoba craftsmen.

Karma | 3,500
Tibet | meters above sea level

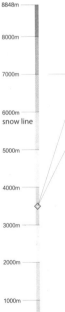

Karma | 3,500
Tibet | meters above sea level

Expanding cities and towns provide more options to people living in the mountains. Nevertheless, they continue in their efforts to carry down their memories through dance, songs, language, costumes, and numerous observances. The culture and religious beliefs of the Qinghai-Tibet Plateau are in part carried down through an important art—the painting of a special kind of scroll called thangka.

Karma Town of Qamdo County is located deep in the mountains where Tibet borders Qinghai. Karma Town is named after the local Karma Gon Monastery, the birthplace of the Karma Kagyu Sect of Tibetan Buddhism. Here the arts of

Smile Like a Bodhisattva: Gama Dele

thangka painting and   Buddhist statue making are handed down from generation to generation.

Karma Gadri, an ancient school of thangka painting, is found in Karma Town which is situated in the Hengduan Mountain Valley. Eighty-two-year-old Gama Dele is a great master of the Karma Gadri tradition. He has painted countless smiling Bodhisattva faces in the past 70 years and has come to smile just like a Bodhisattva. His paintings are like the earth in which one sees profundity, gentleness, and compassion.

In the recent period, the old master and his students have been working overtime to paint a series of fine thangka paintings in order to participate in an exhibition in the holy city of Lhasa. Working and learning with him, his grandchildren have already become outstanding thangka painters.

The preciousness of thangka paintings lies not only in their artistic value but also in the scarce natural pigmcnts used. Unlike chemical paints, these pigments produced from minerals and plants are enduring, thus giving the paintings a longer

life. The colors of a thanka painting remain bright over time, preserving a connection to history.

While they are working at full swing, a stray wounded ox comes by the old man's door. The ox is said to have been bitten by wolves. It limps on its wounded, swollen rear leg, apparently on death's edge.

The old man puts aside his work and checks the ox's wound that is already turning black. With a sorrowful and compassionate look the old man caresses the ox and decides to save it.

The students cannot understand why their master stops his work to save an ox while the team is pressed for time. "Helping those in need is good karma," says the old man. "We should care for others. That's what the Buddha teaches us."

Since highland barley is believed to have antiseptic effects, the old man asks his students to reap some of his highland barley before harvest time. The students apply medicinal fluids to the ox's wound and dress it carefully.

The thangka painting project continues. One of the students reports that larvae are growing in the ox's wound, so it must be cleaned every day or the ox's condition will deteriorate. Now they are also taking pity on the ox.

To their dismay, the ox shows no sign of recovery, so the old man decides to gather some medical herbs himself. Their painstaking efforts are paying off: the ox finally recovers and the painting project is about to be completed as planned. The old man gladly checks the students' artworks, comments on their general satisfactoriness, and suggests that meticulous effort should be made on certain details. Now a moth flies into the studio and the old man opens the window to let it go.

The project is completed and the cow has survived her injury. A Bodhisattva-like smile comes over Gama Dele's face.

Thangka

A unique art of the Tibetan people, thangka paintings resemble ancient scroll paintings of central China. Thangka paintings that have survived over the past centuries are mostly related to Bon and Tibetan Buddhism. With extensive reference to Tibetan history, politics, culture, and society, they can be regarded as an encyclopedia of the Tibetan people.

Thangka are usually painted on cotton or paper and then mounted with a facing cloth of silk brocade. A thin cord is attached to a thangka at the top for the purpose of hanging and an elaborately decorated wood rod is attached to its bottom. After being mounted, a Buddhist thangka needs to be empowered by a sutra-reciting lama who also leaves a gold or cinnabar print of his palm on the back of the painting.

Thangka painting is a sophisticated process that involves the use of mineral and plant pigments. These natural paints are bright, enduring, and characteristic of Tibetan art styles. Thangka appear in varying sizes, ranging from less than one square meter to more than ten square meters, but a regular thangka usually measures between one to two square meters.

The all-embracing subject matter of thangka includes historical events, biographies, religious stories, folk customs, folklore, myths, and architecture layouts which represent Tibet's society, politics, economy, culture, religion, and military affairs. Countless thangka have served to document Tibet's civilization, history, and social development.

Thangka paintings feature precise, balanced, elaborate, and detailed composition. The commonly used techniques include meticulous ink outlining and thickly applied pigments. Besides painted thangka, there are also embroidered, brocaded, woven, appliqued, and pearl-strung thangka whose rich textures and three-dimensional appearances bring forth vivid images.

Ngari | 4,500
Tibet | meters above sea level

8848m
8000m
7000m
6000m
snow line
5000m
4000m
3000m
2000m
1000m
500m
200m
0m

Ngari | *4,500*
Tibet | meters above sea level

As the most sparsely populated region in the world, Ngari is a prefecture of Tibet Autonomous Region. It is located in the northern Qinghai-Tibet Plateau at the heart of the Qangtang Plateau where the Himalayas meet the Gangdisê Mountain Range, so it is called "father of all mountains." It is also known as the "headwater of all rivers" because several domestic and international rivers originate here. Granted that Tibet is the Roof of the World, Ngari is the ridgepole of that Roof, and it is the world's closest zone to the sun. Ngari is home to unique highland landscapes of continuous snowy mountains, the vast

CIRCUMAMBULATION:
BODY-MEASURING THE SACRED MOUNTAINS

Earth Forest, numerous lakes, boundless heathland, and roaming wild animals. Ngari is also home to Tibet's most famous sacred mountain Kangrinboqê and sacred lake Mapam Yongtso.

Ngari, the place where the Himalayas, the Gangdisê Mountain Range, and the Har Goolun Range converge, has an average altitude of more than 4,500 meters, a land area of more than 300,000 square kilometers, and a population of more than 100,000. Most of Ngari's territory comprises uninhabited heathland.

In these mountain ranges of Ngari, Mt. Kangrinboqê is the preeminent mountain, meaning the "precious jewel of the snowy mountains" in Tibetan. Standing 6,638 meters over the plateau, it is the main peak of the Gangdisê Mountain Range, the "center of the world" shared by Bon, Tibetan Buddhism, Hinduism, and Jainism. Kangrinboqê is also called the "king of sacred mountains."

Though a commonplace presence compared to the Himalayas, the peak of

Kangrinboqê at 6,638 meters above sea level stands high on the Ngari highland like a great dome or a brilliantly shining crown. It is treated as the most sacred mountain and circumambulated all year round by believers of quite a few religions who come from all corners of the world.

The practitioners believe that taking a single circumambulatory trip of more than 50 kilometers around Kangrinboqê can cleanse one's life-long bad karma, 10 trips can prevent one from falling into hell in a 500-lifetime birth-rebirth cycle, and 100 trips can make one a buddha in eternal nirvana. One circumambulatory trip around Kangrinboqê in the Year of the Horse is equivalent to 13 trips in other years, and that's why there are many more circumambulators here in the Horse Year.

Some choose to circumambulate the sacred mountain in a much more laborious manner—by prostration. A practitioner holds his palms in the "lotus bud" mudra at his mind, mouth, and heart chakra, prostrates, stands up, and walks three steps which cover a distance equivalent to his body height. He repeats these movements until he completes the circumambulation. This is also called full-body prostration. The Tibetan man Tsewang and two of his townsmen have spent 20 days to complete a circumambulatory circuit around Kangrinboqê by prostration.

Most circumambulation routes are located at the altitude of 5,000 meters. These men have crossed the mountain pass at 5,700 meters above sea level by prostrating along the route, moving three steps forward before and after each prostration. Tsewang's two sons are having their summer vacations and are travelling with their father to give him necessary support.

Circumambulators eat simple foods and are too devout to take any shortcut. Before dark, the three men mark today's finishing spot before they pitch their tent for the night. Early the next morning, they take their tent to the new camping site and then return to where they stopped yesterday to continue their prostration.

Tsewang and his townsman say that when they sleep, they feel Kangrinboqê next to their pillow; in the day, they think about Kangrinboqê high up above; as they lie down on their bellies to worship Kangrinboqê, they believe that the sacred mountain will dispel all their illnesses and agonies. They are thus measuring the circumambulation path with their bodies, draining and regaining their energy bit by bit.

After twenty days, Tsewang is back in the city and continues to work as a water delivery man. His customers will invariably invite him to sit down and take a rest if they chance to know that Tsewang has just finished a circumambulation journey. They admire and respect him. Prostration is the most devout way to worship the Buddha, so a prostrating circumambulator is a devotee who deserves people's respect.

The sacred mountains are deeply rooted in Tibet's religions, history, and culture. They embody Tibetan people's culture and beliefs and the spiritual union of man and nature, humans and gods.

Mountain Circumambulation

Mountain circumambulation is a prevalent religious activity in many parts of Tibet. Devout practitioners take mountain circumambulation tours each year.

The mountains circumambulated are sacred mountains, namely the thousand-kilometer-long Gangdisê Mountain Range and its main peak Mt. Kangrinboqê. Tibet's special climate and natural environment attract large numbers of tourists who come from all corners of the world, many of whom also participate in the circumambulatory trips.

Darchen, a small town at the foot of Mt. Kangrinboqê, is where the circumambulation routes start and finish. Once a small village with hardly more than 20 families, the town has grown in size to serve the needs of circumambulators. Many hotels and guesthouses have been built in Darchen to accommodate a growing number of domestic and overseas circumambulators.

There are two routes encircling Kangrinboqê: a longer outer path and a shorter inner one. Most practitioners take the 52-kilometer longer route. Stronger people, especially the locals, can finish the trip in one day while the others need two days to do the same. Those who perform body-length prostration usually spend 10 to 15 days to complete the trek. It takes devotion and perseverance to travel the 52-kilometer distance either by walk or by prostration at 5,000 meters above sea level.

An important part of the circumambulation is to pay homage to Buddha in small monasteries en route, like the Choku Monastery, the Drirapuk Monastery, and the Zutrulpuk Monastery among others.

Pilgrimage

A Tibetan person typically makes a pilgrimage to pay homage to the Buddha, which is an important way for a Tibetan Buddhist to manifest his or her religious belief. Practitioners performing body-length prostration toward the holy city of Lhasa are seen on both broad highways and mountain paths—a unique feature of the Tibetan landscape.

Tibetan Buddhist practitioners perform body-length prostration as the most devout ritualistic way to worship the Buddha. It is a Tibetan Buddhist belief that worshipping of the Buddha involves three karmas at once, namely body (action), speech (mantras), and mind (thought). While performing prostration, a practitioner lies flat on the ground to express "bodily" reverence, recites mantras to express "oral" reverence, and thinks about Buddha all the time to express "mental" reverence.

Prostration is performed in three ways, namely long-distance, short-distance, and same-spot prostrations. Short-distance prostrations are usually performed by a practitioner who spends a few hours to more than ten days moving clockwise along a path around a monastery or a sacred mountain, lake, or relic. Some prostrate on the same spot in or around the main hall of a monastery. The practitioner recites the six-syllable mantra and prostrates on a mat. Same-spot prostration is exactly the same as long- or short-distance prostrations except that the practitioner does not move forward. Many practitioners believe that one should do at least 100,000 prostrations in this lifetime. In particular, prostrating barefooted shows profound devoutness.

Long-distance prostration involves a set of physical movements and positions. A practitioner stands erect, recites a mantra, usually the six-syllable mantra, and brings his hands together in the "lotus bud" mudra. He holds both hands above his head, to his throat, and then to his heart, each movement followed by a step forward. Upon the third step forward, the practitioner parts his hands, kneels down, puts both palms on the ground, prostrates, and touches the ground with his forehead. When performing prostration, the practitioner keeps reciting the six-syllable mantra: "Om mani padme hong." He repeats the above steps along the trek leading to the holy city of Lhasa. After a night's rest, he will continue his prostration from where he stopped the day before without entertaining a thought of cheating. He usually wears palm and knee pads and an apron-like animal hide for protection. Even so, a callus grows on his forehead which touches the ground countless times.

It is said that each movement of prostration has a special meaning. Closing one's hands in the "lotus bud" mudra means to embrace Buddha's doctrines and teachings. Holding both hands in the "lotus bud" mudra over his head and then at his throat and heart means the practitioner becomes one with Buddha in terms of mind, speech, and heart. When prostrating, one should think about and speak out his wishes at the same time in order for them to come true.

Tibet has formed highly interactive relations with other cultures in its cultural-historical development and has become a highly modernized secular society. Tibetan Buddhist followers, however, remain devoted to their religion and adhere to traditional rituals and ceremonies despite the changes in their lifestyles and social roles.

Diyag | 2,900
Tibet | meters above sea level

8848m
8000m
7000m
6000m
snow line
5000m
4000m
3000m
2000m
1000m
500m
200m
0m

Diyag | *2,900*
Tibet | meters above sea level

Located to the northwest of Zanda County, Ngari Prefecture, Tibet, Diyag Township is the lowest-altitude township in Ngari. It is situated on a gentle gradient next to the Elephant River (Langqên Zangbo River) which roars along precipitous cliffs. Diyag is the most beautiful part of Ngari, and Diyag residents are simple and hospitable people.

THE COLOR OF NGARI:
APPLES GROWN IN DIYAG

Hidden in an Ngari heathland is a tree-covered area where red apples are grown. It is a miracle for so common a fruit as the apple to grow here. This green patch in boundless heathlands is particularly valued by the locals. Apple trees growing next to a house become part of the family and have to be taken care of. Diyag apples have thick skins and are pleasantly fragrant and sweet.

Chötzom's orchard is planted on top of a hill. Her apples are the last to ripen in the village because her large orchard is located at a higher altitude. "My kids go to school far away from home," says Chötzom. "They always ask about our apples when they call home. They want to know if the apples have grown large. I can't just live for myself; I need to think about their future because these apple trees are also their property."

Transporting the apples outside the area is a big problem. Although a road has been paved to connect the village with the outside, apple buyers are often thwarted by the long road that winds through treeless mountains. The villagers need their relatives living in cities to help sell most of their apples.

"Do you sell your apples to the company or on the roadside?" Chötzom asks a fellow villager.

"On the roadside. I haven't signed a contract with the company." She answers.

"How do you carry your apples? Will you hire a truck?" asks Chötzom looking concerned.

"Yes, I will."

This is a high-yield year, and the apple output is larger than previous years. If they cannot be sold in time, these apples will have to be used as yak feed.

Worried about her apples, Chötzom falls ill. A doctor administers an intravenous injection to her and advises her not to let the matter of apples affect her diet and sleep.

Apples are glistening red in the leafy treetops. That is the color of Ngari, the color of industrious Ngari women.

Eventually, Chötzom has got in touch with apple buyers. She is calling to tell them that her village can be reached by road, that her apples are ready, and that they can drive directly to her house.

A truck is running on the winding road. Diyag women are busy in the orchards,

singing joyful songs. They pick burning-red apples, carry them downhill in baskets, and then carefully box them. Tended by the women and nurtured by highland soil and sunshine, these apples are deliciously sour and sweet with a lingering aftertaste. Soon the apples will be loaded on the truck and carried to a faraway place.

The apples are going to travel a long way. The wondrous place the apple truck is passing through is called the "Earth Forest." The vast spectacular Earth Forest shines brilliantly under the highland sun. This place used to be a wide lake million years ago. Later, rising mountains lifted the lake basin, and wind and water have reshaped the terrain here.

More than 100,000 people lived here during the Guge dynasties. They even built a horse farm on the Earth Forest. The Guge Kingdom disappeared mysteriously, but the Guge people left behind evidence of their existence. Those ancient murals, weathered by time yet bright as ever, bear witness to Ngari's past glory. The dances depicted in the murals, dating back 1,000 years, originated in the land of apples.

The "Third Pole" is the peak of all mountains and the headwater of great rivers. It is the harmonious home of numerous creatures.

The Earth Forest of Zanda

The Earth Forest of Zanda is an example of terrain formed by soil erosion. It features column-like soil deposits which look like a forest from a distance, hence its name. Geologically, this is called fluvial-lacustrine sedimentation resulted from geological changes which took place a million years ago.

With a total area of 2,464 square kilometers, the Earth Forest of Zanda is located in Zanda County, Ngari, Tibet. It is the largest and most typical earth forest among all its peers which have been formed by virtue of Tertiary crustal erosion.

Zanda in Tibetan means a "grassy lower reach." According to geological findings, there used to be a vast lake measuring more than 500 square kilometers between Zanda and Burang one million years ago. The Himalayan tectonics raised the lake basin and caused the waterline to drop. In the dry, cold climate, the exposed lake bottom was eroded by seasonal water currents to form crisscross ravines. The standing rocks began to assume wondrous looks thanks to long-term exposure to wind and rain. Ultimately, after a million years of "carving" and "chiseling," the precipitous rocky cliffs and columns have come to resemble variously shaped majestic castles and grand fortresses. They constitute one of nature's masterpieces and are the best known landscape of Ngari. In 2007, the Zanda Earth Forest became a national level geopark.

Such special natural landscapes as stone forests, earth forests, and ice spire forests are seen everywhere in China's vast territory. Earth forests are found in Yunnan, Sichuan, Gansu, and Xinjiang, but the Zanda Earth Forest against a highland background of blue sky and snowy mountains stands out as a unique spectacle. It shows nature's superb craftsmanship and presents traces of an epoch-spanning process. In the Zanda Earth Forest one finds many fresco and grotto relics; one will also see palace and monastery ruins of the once powerful Guge Kingom. The Zanda Earth Forest is a unique combination of human architecture and special geological features.

The Guge Kingdom

Ancient ruins of the Guge Kingdom are located on the mountaintop next to the Elephant River 18 kilometers away from Zanda County, Ngari. Covering a total area of 180,000 square meters, it is listed among China's first group of "national key cultural relic protection sites." The ruins in this architectural complex comprise stupas, monasteries, palace halls, and more than 300 grottos. The palace halls and monasteries are situated on the highest point of the Earth Forest, and down from the hilltop are respectively residential homes and grottos. City walls have been built at the foot of the hill with four watchtowers standing on four corners. Beautiful murals and exquisite Buddha statues are still extant in the palace halls and monasteries on top of the hill.

The Guge Kingdom played an important role in Tibetan History. It was a local regime established by descendants of the Tubo Kingdom, and its territory included all of Ngari in its prime. Upon reaching the peak of its historical development, it not only served to continue the Tubo royal genealogy but also sheltered Buddhist traditions after the demise of the Tubo Kingdom.

Established in the middle of the 10th century, the Guge Kingdom eventually collapsed in the early 1600s. Sixteen Guge kings ruled over West Tibet for more than 700 years.

The first westerners to reach Guge were the Portuguese Jesuit Father António de Andrade and his companion Brother Manuel Marques, in 1626. They settled down and evangelized in Guge.

Once a brilliant civilization, the Guge Kingdom mysteriously disappeared after 1630. No written record of the Guge Kingdom has been discovered so far.

Nothing about its disappearance is heard among the Tibetan residents who have been living here for generations. What the mysterious kingdom has left behind are the lonely ruins of a castle and the sculptures, carvings, and frescos in and around it.

Many assumptions have been made about the Guge Kingdom's mysterious disappearance. Two theories are widely acknowledged by academia.

One theory favors religious reasons. After the demise of the Tubo regime, Tibet disintegrated into warring states. Guge needed manpower and financial resources to fight against its neighboring states. Under growing influences of Buddhism, however, many war-aversive Tibetans had by now chosen to lead monastic lives in monasteries, which contributed to the shortage of military troops. Constantly beset by outside forces, the pro-Christian king of Guge conscripted lamas into the army. This resulted in a chasm between the Christian ruler and the Tibetan Buddhist leaders, and the ensuing insurgences by armed lamas ultimately toppled the Guge Kingdom.

The other theory is grounded in environmental reasons. The Guge king ruled over a large territory in Ngari with 100,000 subjects living on this fertile land. Yet prolonged dry spells began to change the environment as fertile enclaves disappeared and desertification dealt a fatal blow on Guge's agriculture and husbandry. The farmers and herdsmen were forced to leave their homes, and the once-mighty Guge Kingdom fell into decline.

The prime relics found in the Guge ruins are murals which have been preserved in good condition. Impressive with their grand composition and unique style, these murals not only depict Buddhist deities but also represent real-life figures and daily scenes ranging from kings and ambassadors to monks and laymen, from court servants to people on the street, from religious rituals to festive celebrations. The wide-ranging themes of the murals are vivid representations of the various aspects of the Guge society.

Realistic in style, Guge murals are highly decorative with fine lines and thick bright colors. The paints used were made by mixing yak gelatin with mineral and plant pigments, so the colors of the murals are not only pure but also durable and bright. That's why the Guge murals have remained colorful as ever over the past millennium, manifesting an esthetic taste for simplicity and sincerity.

The
ཀ༄།འཛིན་སྐྱིང་ Third
ཡང་ཆེ།། Pole

THERE IS NO HIERARCHY OF JOBS
AT DÊGÊ PARKHANG:
EVEN SWEEPING THE FLOOR IS A
REWARD FOR ONE'S GOOD KARMA
OF THE PREVIOUS LIFE.

MEETING ON THE PLATEAU

This documentary is about the relationship between man and nature on the Qinghai-Tibet Plateau. It required more than courage and enthusiasm to shoot this documentary.

The shooting of this film was commenced on Sept. 29th, 2013. In the ensuing year, six research teams and four camera crews traveled across the Plateau, covering a total distance of more than 100,000 kilometers and working a total number of 500 crew-days. Our editors worked a total of 200 days on its post-production. In the filming phase, the crew worked efficiently despite many challenges, such as altitude sickness, frequent change of location, inadequate road access, illnesses, malfunctioning drones, and difficulties with food and accommodation. Yet they also enjoyed many pleasant surprises provided by nature.

An important part of the preliminary work was to record the life of black-necked cranes. Through much research the crew decided to start filming in spring when large numbers of the birds bred their young. They proceeded with their plan and searched about in the birds' reputed habitat. There were many bird species in sight but the black-necked cranes were nowhere to be found. They could only turn to the local herdsmen who told them that the cranes' breeding site was no more than a dark speck in the middle of a lake. Flocks of black-necked cranes were a usual sight on the plateau, but these birds would hide themselves in the breeding season. After many days, with the help of local herdsmen and the forestry department, the crew eventually found traces of black-necked cranes near the lake.

The black-necked cranes were vigilant birds which might give alarm calls at the sight of any human activity in the distance. The crew could only hide themselves in a tent with their equipment and wait around the clock for opportunities to film the

cranes. That required extraordinary patience, but they felt greatly gratified when they managed to film the birds going about their activities.

The most outstanding feature of the "Third Pole" is its high elevation. We chose to film at Tui Village, over 5,000 meters above sea level, in order to understand how people lived at such an extreme altitude. The environment of Tui Village posed a test not only to the local people's subsistence strategies but also our preparedness to work there.

Our decision to film at Pumo Yongtso went against the usual scheduling for visits to the plateau, but we had no choice as there was no telling when the sheep would cross the frozen lake. Whenever it was to happen, it would be one of the coldest days in a year. Working on the cold highland, everyone felt themselves being pushed to their limit. Some of us fell ill due to extreme physical stress. The

temperature dropped below minus 20 degrees Celsius when the filming began. Working several days on end, most of the crew began to feel sick and exhausted, and silence replaced the initial excitement.

Altitudes above 5,000 meters are unsuitable for human habitation, but the locals are used to the high-elevation environment. The crew members, mostly from China's interior, were constantly challenged by the high altitudes. Oxygen content of the highland winter air was only 60% of the normal level. The challenge posed to flatlanders by such conditions was equivalent to carrying a 40- to 60-kilo load. Pumo Yongtso is a sizeable lake where the crew had to walk 5 to 6 kilometers on ice every day. They probably had never worked in such harsh environment.

Tui villagers availed themselves of the frozen lake to herd their sheep, including pregnant ewes, to islands where the sheep could graze on lush pastures. In order to represent the story from a special perspective, the crew used underwater filming beneath ice. According to the cameraman, there had been no precedent of underwater filming on highlands. The pressure one felt at 5 to 6 meters under water was equivalent to that at the sea level, so coming out of the water was equivalent to stepping right onto an altitude of 5,000 meters. Besides such obvious danger, other

unexpected situations could have arisen at any time, so the crew had to be extremely careful.

Environmental complexities led to technical difficulties, and some filming devices were rendered unusable. The drones, for example, could not take off, so the crew had to give up aerial filming over Pumo Yongtso.

High altitude represented only a small portion of the difficulties confronting the crew. Vegetation was lush in Himalaya mountain valleys at lower altitudes, but there

were other dangers involved. People there lived a vastly different life due to features of the local setting. Some of them would even risk their lives to gather honeycombs.

Cliff climbing was a normal thing for the Sherpas but posed a great challenge to the camera crew. A rock climbing expert from Yangshuo, Guangxi, was hired to work as the cameraman. The crew was divided into four groups: the rock climber would film the honey gatherer, another cameraman would film Sherpas in the woods, a third cameraman would use telephoto lenses to capture close-up images, and the aerial filming team would film the interactions between people and the environment.

The rock climber had to move close enough to the beehive to film it, but the bees noticed and attacked him. Those were the largest bees in the world, and 3 or 4 stings could have killed someone allergic to bee venom. The Sherpas finally succeeded in lighting a torch, but as they were ready to smoke out the bees, an accident happened: the drone went out of control and fell into the river below. That was one of the most dangerous moments. We were hardly prepared for such dangers and difficulties, but the crew managed to film the entire honey gathering process, thus demonstrating the inhabitants' courage and knowhow.

As the crew moved ahead with the project, they encountered more difficulties resulting from the harsh environment. The crew left Mêdog, the last county in China to have road access, and went into remoter mountains where horses and mules had to be hired to carry our equipment and supplies.

It was raining as the crew climbed the precipitous cliffs next to the Yarlung Zangbo River to film soapstone pot making in Mêdog. The road was in worse condition on their way back and mudslides and landslides were seen everywhere. One of the vehicles got into trouble, with one-fourth of its length hanging off a cliff. They could only unload it and then pull it back onto the road.

Continuous mountains form the backdrop of the "Third Pole," where the inhabitants have dwelled generation after generation. The filming process was full of hardships, but what the crew members would recall was those many memorable moments, those fascinating behind-the-scene stories. The crew felt the magnanimity of the "Third Pole" as they travelled from cities to deserts, from mountains to grasslands, from rivers to forests.

The crew traveled a lot, spending about one-fourth of their time on the road. They might be working in the forest in the morning and arriving at a heathland in the evening; they might be filming animals on the grassland one day and be back in the city the next day. Developed highways of the Qinghai-Tibet Plateau largely reduced their time spent on traveling, and the crew could reach any chosen location along those roads. There were amazing landscapes along the highway which were too beautiful to be missed. The crew would keep their eyes open for the natural beauties unless sometimes they desperately needed a brief power nap.

They met a Tibetan medical doctor who was distressed by a minor malfunction in his iPad. His clinic, a grotto, was said to be a thousand years old. He had a wide range of electronic devices and used internet access to study medicinal substances he needed. Though living on the heathland, he didn't feel lonely. The crew members were interested in his way of life as his experiences and lifestyle embodied a combination of ancient Tibetan traditions and modern developments.

While embracing a modern lifestyle, people paid increased attention to the protection of their traditional culture. Tsering Dorji was a propagator of Tibetan paper making as an non-material cultural heritage. The distinctive features of his Tibetan paper came from the poisonous spurge roots he used. Manually collected spurge roots were far from enough for large-scale paper making, but few people were willing to dig spurge roots in the mountains because of their increased living standards. Tsering Dorji used modern machines to plow a patch of farm land and was finally able to grow spurge in large quantities.

The highlanders had a consensus about preservation of their traditional culture, and that's why Sitar Dorji, a King Gesar epic bard, became a special enrolled student at Tibet University, even though most King Gesar bards had been illiterate in old times.

The director said that Sitar Dorji appeared to be a regular college student like anyone else, except that he talked about King Gesar once in a while. As he sat down before the camera in the studio, however, he changed back into a traditional epic singer. It was amazing to see him switch between such contrasting roles. Sitar Dorji was soon to graduate from Tibet University, but he chose to stay to continue with his studies on the epic King Gesar.

Pounding aga was a traditional Tibetan architectural technology used to build roofs and floors. It was a pleasant job combining singing and dancing. The aga pounding we filmed was no different from such occasions in any other part of Tibet except that the young people contributed a modern look to it. The joyous youngsters looked just like a group of teenagers dancing on the street, only they were dancing more passionately under the highland sun.

There was also a modern cast to the vitality found at Mindroling Monastery, the oldest Buddhist temple in Tibet. The young monks, a group of sometimes mischievous students, worked devotedly under the guidance of their masters to make a sand mandala depicting the Buddha's cosmos. The process of sand mandala making had been kept confidential due to considerations of preserving the heritage. This time, however, the monks were very tolerant and allowed the crew to film the entire process of sand mandala making, including its final destruction. It took the monks a long time to make the mandala but only one minute to destroy it. Besides its religious implications, the destruction of the mandala could serve as a metaphor for the passing away of all temporal things.

A special environment shaped the highlanders' characters. Such epithets as vivacious, simple, and serious are not enough to describe them; deep inside, they are kind-hearted and compassionate.

Having filmed black-necked cranes, the crew passed by a herdsman's tent on their way back. The matron gave them a hospitable treat. A little creature showed up as everyone was enjoying the delicious food. It was one of the six wolf puppies the herdsman had adopted while herding their cattle. Their hearts had melted when they saw the pitiful puppies, the herdsmen said, but they hated the prospect of the puppies growing up someday into sheep-eating adults.

Wolves had attacked their sheep only a few days before, so the way they treated the wolf puppies was quite unexpected. The crew learned about the puppies but didn't know how to begin to film the story. Then they happened to find out that some herdsmen had called the police because more than 20 of their sheep had just suffered a wolf attack. It was surprising to see the shepherds feeding the pups with

the remaining flesh of a sheep killed by wolves. Yet one could not help being touched by a harmonious relationship between humans and animals, as manifested by this kindhearted act.

The crew heard about an old man in Lhasa who practiced circumambulation with his sheep, so they managed to find this man. People's lifestyle had largely changed by then and only a few individuals would think of doing circumambulation with a sheep like the old man did. The elders among the people, however, would like to persist in such a way of life.

The old man brought his sheep with him when he took a circumambulation trip or visited relatives. When the old man drank sweet tea in the teahouse, the sheep would stand close to him, silently looking at people and things around it, as if it had already become a part of a social milieu. Filming the story of the old man and his sheep, the crew got the chance to know about the Lhasa people's everyday life and celebrated the Tibetan New Year with them.

At Tangra Yongtso, Tibet, people celebrated the Spring Plowing Festival. Although the filming focused on the festivities, two 80-year-old twin sisters added highlights to the story. The crew filmed them for only two days. The lovely sisters whispered to each other in front of the camera. The crew knew nothing about what they said but later got to know that they were talking about the filming. "What a tiring job it is!" said one to the other. "It's better to do dharma practice."

Chief cinematographer Sun Shaoguang said that he had seen all kinds of people in his filming career, but the Tibetan experience had been the most memorable part. The Tibetan people were very friendly and tolerant with the crew and their cameras. They simply acted as usual despite the presence of the crew, doing what they were doing and saying whatever came to their mind. That was the best situation a documentary crew could ever hope for.

Traveling on the Qinghai-Tibet Plateau, the crew members were expecting surprises, but they were often touched by the sincere smiles of the Tibetan people. What they saw most of the time were familiar things which manifested the everlasting qualities of devoutness, benevolence, simplicity, and tenacity.

The
Third
Pole

ༀ།།འཛིན་སྐྱོང་
ཡར་ཅིི།

WE HAVE BOTH GROWN ANOTHER
YEAR OLDER.
I WISH WE CAN BE STILL TOGETHER
THIS TIME NEXT YEAR. I WISH WE
CAN LIVE A HUNDRED YEARS TO
SEE MORE OF FALL HARVESTS.

Behind-the-Scenes Stories

Lovely Ladies

Many viewers of *The Third Pole* are amazed to see so many lovely ladies on the Qinghai-Tibet Plateau: they do not wear makeup but their beauty is all the more striking for its purity.

The Most Beaming Smiles

The altitude of the "Third Pole" bespeaks the high-mindedness of people living on the Qinghai-Tibet Plateau. Their cheerful faces are pure and natural, their smiles full of love and happiness.

The Cutest Animals

In *The Third Pole* one sees dozens of animals: black-necked crane, snow leopard, fox, wolf, antelope, wild donkey, yak, macaque, mastiff, horse, bee, pika, etc., all of which have close interchanges with humans. They make you smile and melt your heart.

Afterword

Production of *The Third Pole:* An Interview with Cinematographer
Sun Shaoguang

The Third Pole is a large-scale documentary series recently released to wide acclaim. Produced in 4K resolution, it is the first ever Chinese documentary to give a panoramic account of the harmonious coexistence of man and nature on the Qinghai-Tibet Plateau.

Sun Shaoguang, cinematographer and director of photography of *The Third Pole*, also worked as cinematographer on the documentaries *Last Train Home* and *China Heavyweight*. He is a winner of the Documentary Emmys, the "Evans Award" of International Documentary Film Festival Amsterdam, and Taiwan's Golden Horse "Best Documentary" award.

The following is the transcription of a dialogue between Sun Shaoguang and Huang Qian from the HOMEBOY CINE STUDIO, who worked as colorist for *The Third Pole*:

Huang: First let's talk about the camera. My first impression of *The Third Pole*, upon getting the rough cut, was that the light was strong throughout this documentary, though it was made in a challenging environment. Did you make any specific filming plan? Did you compare cameras before making a choice? Did the pictures turn out to be what you had expected?

Sun: My choice of camera was based on the director's requirements: 4K resolution, high-speed shooting feature, and within budget. Cameras available on the market at the end of 2013 when the shooting began were the F55, RED, and C500. The F55 was a good camera but didn't have a built-in high-speed shooting feature. C500 on the other hand needed an exterior recorder; its RAW storage format and the postproduction procedure involved would be costly and complicated. Also I didn't choose it because it was not upgradeable. The F65 and ALEXA could produce fine pictures but were not an option, because they fell short in terms of ease of operation for documentary making. I chose RED in the end.

RED is an unlikely choice when you think of all the advanced cameras made today, because it doesn't have a built-in ND. To enhance its operation, we had to use filters and a lens hood, which reduced its portability. The sunlight in Tibet was so strong that overexposure was unavoidable even if we minimized ISO. We had to use minimum aperture, say between 22 and 30, but that resulted in diffraction which reduced the clarity of the pictures. Other problems included magenta cast under high luminance, poor performance under low luminance, and high signal-to-noise ratio (ISO at 1600) that affected the pictures. Despite Tibet's strong sunlight, indoor light was very dim. We couldn't use a combination of lighting techniques because we were

making a documentary. Where there was no electricity, we had to use a campfire and portable energy-saving lamps. Those were the factors that affected the quality of the pictures. Another weakness of RED was that there was no protective lens to shield its CMOS from dust in Tibet's harsh environment. We used pressurized nitrogen to blow off the dust, but the effects were limited because of Tibet's high altitude. As a result, we had to be extremely careful when changing lenses.

The RED was nevertheless a good choice because of its relatively developed RAW compatibility for editing, plus its high-speed shooting feature. In fact, the editing requirement was also an important factor. I took into consideration suggestions both from the editor and the colorist. The editor advised me on the storage, editing, and cost-effectiveness of different formats. My decision was also informed by recommendations of the colorist who would tell me how much room for adjustment there was for a certain segment. He would tell me about problems with the pictures, and I could immediately figure out the technical performance of the camera while shooting scenes. If I were to make the choice today, I might choose the Amira or F55 because they are easily portable and adaptable. They have perfect audio function and are calibrated for a wide range of lenses. These features are ideal for making documentaries.

Sun: We thought it over and decided not to use the PL adaptor, because what we would be using most of the time were zoom lenses instead of fixed-focus lenses. The PL adaptor's allowable zoom range wouldn't be adequate if we were to film a scene by carrying the camera on the shoulder, and that would reduce efficiency dramatically. That's why we used the Canon EF most of the time. We used the Sigma 300-800mm zoom lens to film wild animals and the 5D to capture single frames. Unlike film camera lenses, these lenses could not produce balanced and consistent pictures, and subtle differences existed among lenses of different brands, but their strong points were suitable for documentary filmmaking. These lenses have high performance-price ratios, they are portable and adaptable, and replacements are easily available even if they are damaged in harsh environment. In Tibet, the most difficult part was filming the sky which was so bright that overexposure was hard to avoid. We used graduated ND filters and chose suitable angles where possible to avoid overexposure. But what counts is what the documentary tells about, so the inadequacies of the pictures are acceptable in my view.

Huang: As a senior cinematographer who's won many awards for your documentaries, how did you work collaboratively with the film director?

Sun: In fact we had many interactions during the filming process; we discussed our impressions of the shots and segments. The director liked serene and spacious scenes; we would view what we filmed during the day to discuss if adjustments were needed. In fact, the role of the cinematographer is equivalent to that of the storyboard director, but my filming was largely based on intuition. That was risky to some extent because my aesthetic pointedly informed the film; it was a double-edged weapon. I believe that the director trusted me because he gave me much room to work freely. I understood what he had in mind through our conversations, so I could quickly translate his ideas into visual symbols.

Huang: What were the major difficulties in the two-year production of *The Third Pole*? What did you do to handle them?

Sun: As far as my job was concerned, the major problem was the high altitude: we felt exhausted. It was crucial to define our respective jobs in order to avoid confusion which might make our job more exhausting. The harsh environment was another challenge. One day the cable was broken because of cold weather, and we had to drive four hours to find a soldering iron. And the drones couldn't work properly under low air pressure. We concluded that it was important to understand the equipment's operative temperature range before starting filming in an extreme environment.

Huang: Today the era of acetate film is soon coming to an end while digital technology is predominant. How do you look at the choice between digital tape and acetate film?

Sun: I was not optimistic about digital technology in its initial stage. My assumption was that it could only produce poor low-pixel pictures. With celluloid film manufacturing giants going bankrupt one after another, however, I soon realized that I was wrong. Digital technology has not been able to simulate some of the unique qualities produced by chemical reactions while developing celluloid film, but I believe technical breakthroughs will be achieved in the future. We should never rule out technical innovations, and it is important to try new things. A new generation of cinematographers has come to the fore precisely because new technologies ended the predominance of celluloid film. On the whole, I am optimistic about the future of digital technologies.

Huang: You were unable to work personally with us on the coloring of the film, but how do you look at the collaboration between the cinematographer and the colorist in the digital era?

Sun: It is vital for the cinematographer to participate in the coloring process because he can share what he felt about the scenes with the colorist. Yet it is also important to leave more space for the colorist because collaboration based on mutual trust often brings about surprises. I myself am familiar with the RAW format which frees the cinematographer from concerns about white balance and color temperature and gives much space for postproduction. In making a documentary, three measurements are enough: 5500 K or 6000 K on overcast and fine days and 3200 K in a low luminance environment or under lamplight. Occasional color casts are acceptable because colors can express sentiments and a sense of temporality. Moreover, high-speed data flow allows for modifications and adjustments, and one needs to ensure that this aspect is not lost. As I was monitoring the use of the Red gamma3 on the spot, I did not pay much attention to the aspect of color. Instead, I used the histogram as a guide for exposure. Today, the colorist is increasingly participating in the filming process to give the director and cinematographer suggestions on the pictures. This is becoming a standard practice where postproduction expertise plays a part in the filming process.

Huang: As a much acclaimed senior documentary cinematographer, how do you balance your career and personal life?

Sun: This is in fact a romantic job that allows you to travel to many places, to see interesting people and things, and to get a better understanding of the world. I am not biased against commercials or commercial movies because they expose me to new ideas, technologies, and equipment and help keep my expertise up to date. Making a documentary, however, is more about meeting challenges in an uncontrollable environment; it means to know about the world, so it is something useful for society. For my part, to be a cinematographer is a choice second to none. Everything is gained at the loss of something else; I enjoy what I have gained, so I let the other things run their course.

Huang: Last but not least, what suggestions do you have for young people who plan to work as documentary filmmakers?

Sun: In fact, China's documentary filmmaking has a strong demand for cinematographers who know how to tell stories and who have a good control of scenes. The more experienced a cinematographer is, the more valuable his expertise will be. Young people planning to work as documentary filmmakers need lots of enthusiasm and patience to achieve their life goals. They will go through a long process filled with alternating loneliness and happiness. Of course they can also voice their requests for equitable treatment and recognition in the movie industry.

The Third Pole

Produced by	CCTV Chinese International Channel
	Beijing Five Star Legend Culture Company
Supervised by	State Council Information Office
Producers	Guo Xin, Nie Chenxi
Project Developers	Qi Ju, Wei Dichun
General Supervisor	Ren Xue'an
Supervisor	Ma Yong
General Production Heads	Wang Weilai, Yan Zhanling
Production Head	Hu Xiaolu
Production Chiefs	Du Xing, Hu Mage
Director of Photography	Sun Shaoguang
Cinematography	Sun Shaoguang, Xie Zhuoliang, An Tongqing, Ren Jie, Dekar, Wang Qin
Theme Music	S.E.N.S.
Song by	Xu Wei
Music	Yutaka Takezawa, Eiji Mori, Yang Guanglei
Director of Recording	Qi Hui
Director of Editing	Zhang Kaifa
Co-directors	Wen Pei, Qiao Sen, An Tongqing, Zhang Hongsong
Text Compiler	Xiao Henggang
Chief Director	Zeng Hairuo

The Third Pole

Acknowledgements (names listed in no particular order)

Zhou Bin, Xu Li, Yang Lijun, Che Gang, Gyatso, Zhang Tongdao, He Suliu, Lu Zhi, Zhang Lixian, Dong Wenjun, Liu Jianqiang, Gao Xiulan, Khamtru Rinpoche, Tang Jie, Yuan Hong, Hu Jiujiu, Lobsang Tsering, Ren Changzhen, Kogcho Rinpoche, Xu Jian, Mou Zhengpeng, Liu Yanlin, Huang Yong, Wu Yuchu, Qiao Qiao, Luo Jingmin, Luo Hao, Zhao Xiaoyan, Feng Xiang, Zhang Xiaobei, Zhou Tiedong, Mou Sen, Gao Xiaolong, Sichuan Provincial Bureau of Tourism, Banma Creative Media, Huiming Culture

Chief Partner
Volvo Automobile China

Science Consultancy
Chinese Academy of Sciences, Institute of Tibetan Plateau Research

Academic Support Institutions
Chinese Academy of Social Sciences
China Tibetology Research Center
Academy of Social Sciences of Tibet Autonomous Region

Facilitators
The People's Government of Tibet Autonomous Region
The People's Government of Qinghai Province
The People's Government of Sichuan Province
The People's Government of Gansu Province
The People's Government of Yunnan Province
Tibet TV Station
Lhasa Municipal Bureau of Tourism

Online Social Media
SinaMicroblog@documentarythethirdpole
WeChat Public Number: documentarythethirdpole (QR code)

We extend our special thanks to all those who have rendered support to the making of this documentary!

图书在版编目（CIP）数据

第三极：英文/郭新编；王浩译. -- 北京：
五洲传播出版社，2015.5
ISBN 978-7-5085-3162-5

Ⅰ.①第… Ⅱ.①郭… ②王… Ⅲ.①电视纪录片 –
解说词 – 中国 – 当代 – 英文 Ⅳ.①I235.2

中国版本图书馆CIP数据核字(2015)第103384号

出 版 人：荆孝敏
统　　筹：付　平
审　　稿：张　云
翻　　译：王　浩
英文审稿：Denis Mair
发行总监：张　斌
特邀编辑：宋舒虹
责任编辑：张美景
图片提供：北京五星传奇文化传媒有限公司
装帧设计：北京正视文化艺术有限责任公司
设计总监：闫志杰
装帧设计：徐　驰
设计制作：魏向东

第三极

出版发行：五洲传播出版社
社　　址：北京市海淀区北三环中路31号生产力大楼B座7层
邮政编码：100088
网　　址：http://www.cicc.org.cn
电　　话：0086-010-82007837（发行部）
印　　刷：北京卡乐富印刷有限公司
开　　本：787mm×1092mm 1/16
字　　数：100千字
印　　张：17
版　　次：2015年8月第1版第1次印刷
定　　价：139.00元